Leadership Rules

50 Timeless Lessons For Leaders

Jo Owen

CAPSTONE

This edition first published 2011
© 2011 Jo Owen

Registered office
Capstone Publishing Ltd. (A Wiley Company), The Atrium, Southern
Gate, Chichester, West Sussex, PO19 8SQ, United Kingdom

For details of our global editorial offices, for customer services and for
information about how to apply for permission to reuse the copyright
material in this book please see our website at www.wiley.com.

The right of the author to be identified as the author of this work has been
asserted in accordance with the Copyright, Designs and Patents Act 1988.

Library of Congress Cataloguing-in-Publication Data
••

A catalogue record for this book is available from the British Library.

9780857082381 (paperback)   9780857082442 (epdf)
9780857082459 (epub)   9780857082466 (emobi)

Set in 12/18pt Times New Roman PS by Toppan Best-set Premedia
Limited

Printed and bound in Great Britain by TJ International Ltd. Padstow,
Cornwall, UK

Illustrations by Mackerel

CONTENTS

WHAT'S NEW ABOUT LEADERSHIP

INTRODUCTION

When you next go to the office, try the following exercise. Throw away your mobile phone. Unplug your computer and get rid of any internet connections. Tell all the staff functions that their services are no longer required: out goes IT, HR, finance, accounting and legal services. Get rid of all the consultants. While you are about it, you may as well cut off the electricity and water supply.

Now try leading.

Modern creature comforts go from luxury to necessity faster than ever before. As leaders, we are becoming surrounded by ever more sophisticated corporate life support systems. We cannot imagine how we lived or led without modern technology, support and staff. Leadership has become a gilded cage: the rewards may be great, but we depend more and more on the system to function effectively.

If we want to rediscover the essence of leadership we have to escape the gilded cage and go back to basics. To do this, we have to look at leaders who have led without the benefit of an MBA, Power-Point and the latest smart phone. Fortunately, we do not need to travel far. We can travel a little way back in history to see how leaders succeeded with far fewer resources than we have today.

Another way of travelling back in time is to visit the remaining traditional societies of the world. At first sight, it may appear that we have nothing to learn from leaders who stick feathers in their hair and bones through their noses. But, for a moment, let's compare how they have fared compared to the great leaders of the modern business world. If we go back one generation we find that the creation of the FTSE 100. It represented the biggest and best of British business. They were the firms and the leaders we were meant to aspire to become. So how many of these great titans of business are still in the FTSE 100? Just 28. The other 72 have been taken over, overtaken or gone plain bust. A similar story can be told if you look at the S&P 500 in the United States or the Fortune Global 100. For all the brilliance of the great business leaders we read about in articles and autobiographies, they have an astonishing failure rate. A tribe which lasted only one generation would not be very successful. Most of the tribes I studied have lasted hundreds of years: that is, further back than anyone could remember.

So we find that tribes last much longer, in far harsher conditions with far fewer resources than the modern business tribe. Maybe, just maybe, we can learn something from their success. For sure, we need to take a fresh look at leadership. Look at some of the top selling books on business and leadership recently. *Good to Great* did extensive research to find those firms which had discovered the essence of lasting success. Since then the fate of the 11 American-only firms they studied has been less than stellar. Nucor issued its first profit warning; Gillette got taken over; Fannie Mae got bailed out for over $100 billion; and Circuit City went plain bust. So much for conventional success formulas.

The research for this book is based on seven years of working and living with tribes from Mali to Mongolia, from the Arctic to Australia via Papua New Guinea and beyond to see how they are led. Their survival and success is a small miracle. They have minimal resources. They often live in the most inhospitable areas, from frozen tundra to jungles, and are often surrounded by other hostile tribes. These tribes have survived for hundreds of years.

They show us the essence of leadership through the ages; leadership without all the noise of modern life. Throughout the book, the lessons of traditional leadership stand in contrast to modern leadership practice, observed from working with over 100 of the best, and a few of the worst, organisations on our planet. This is supplemented with original leadership research conducted mainly in the UK, USA and France, but supported by experience of working in most continents and most industries.

This research shows that the nature of leadership changes around the world. Something odd happens to leaders when they cross from Dover to Calais: different assumptions come into play. And if we then go further afield to the Middle East, or Asia, the assumptions change even more. This should stop us and make us take notice. Most leadership books are written on the assumption that the Anglo-Saxon, specifically American, way is the only way. Classic books like *In Search of Excellence* and *Good to Great* do not bother to examine non-American ways of leading. Such insularity is not good. Anyone who has cared to go to Beijing or Bangalore will quickly see that there is another world getting ready to take over from the American way. So we need to reach beyond the conventional formulas of Anglo-Saxon leadership if we are to survive, let alone succeed.

Going around the world in search of the essence of leadership was a recipe for dizziness. Even within one country, each leader was very clear about the essence of leadership. But each leader had a completely different formula for success. Across countries and continents, the differences simply grew. The fog of confusion descended. But perhaps the fog teaches us a couple of lessons. First, there is no single formula for success. If there was, you could programme a computer and ask it to lead: perhaps we will get to that stage one day. Each leader makes their own success formula, and they do what it takes to succeed in their unique context. So that leads to a second rule: you have to find the context in which your unique strengths will flourish: Churchill was great in war and useless in peace. The same leader in different contexts achieves different outcomes. The third rule from the fog is that no leader gets ticks in all the boxes. None of the leaders I interviewed was perfect, and they knew it. You do not need to be perfect. But you do need to grow your unique talents and make sure you are in the right place to use them well.

Ultimately, the purpose of working with both tribes and businesses was to discover what, if anything, successful leaders have in common. If certain skills and habits are essential in both the boardroom and the bush, then we can be fairly sure that they are universal traits of leadership. They are not simply an Anglo-Saxon take on leadership. And the positive outcome was that there were common themes, even if there was no single formula for success.

And now for the good news. More or less everything that is expected of a leader can be learned. You do not have to have the right DNA and the right parents to be a good leader. The expectations of a good leader can be grouped into three parts, which represent the first three sections of this book.

First, there are some universal qualities that leaders should have. Tribal societies in particular look at the qualities of the person, not just their technical skills. The importance of this was emphasised by one modern-day CEO who said: "I find I hire most people for their technical skills and fire most for their lack of values or people skills." Fortunately, most of the qualities of a leader can be learned. Tribes talked about courage being important: modern CEOs also talk about courage to take the tough decisions. In working with the fire service and army, it became clear that even physical courage can be learned.

The second section of the book looks at the skills a leader must master. Again, there is no magic here. Decision making, taking control, managing people are all skills that any leader can learn and every leader must learn. The real challenge is how you learn these skills. Here there was a unanimous verdict from both tribes and businesses: experience is everything. That raises the obvious challenge of how you get the right experience and accelerate your learning from it.

The third section of the book looks at what leaders must do. Again, there is a common theme all the way from Papua New Guinea to Paris. Leaders have to take people where they would not have got by themselves. Managers administer a legacy and keep things running: they are essential in any society. But to lead, you need to do more. The one message that came through loud and clear was: "change or die". In the business world, this is a rhetorical message. In the tribal world it is a literal message: without change they perish. Living on the edge gives an intensity and purpose to everything. Tribal people are often change masters.

Clearly, the tribal world does not enjoy the luxuries that we take for granted: running water, electricity, food, rule of law and relative peace. Something has stopped them progressing. The fourth section looks at what stops their progress: the problem is not one of leadership. This section is a chance to relish all those things that enable our progress but which we take for granted.

Finally, it would be unrealistic to pretend that nothing has changed about leadership in the last few thousand years. Things have changed. So the fifth and final section of the book looks at what is new about leadership. The results are mixed. The good news is that now anyone can become a leader, and that leadership is no longer about your title. It is about how you perform: you do not need to be a king or CEO before you start leading. The bad news is that many leaders have become very confused about leadership: they are in position, but they are not in power. They are not leading. And in too many cases, they have come to believe that leadership is about how you can help yourself, not how you can help others.

This book does not pretend to be a leadership manual. It simply holds up a mirror to modern leadership practices and invites you to draw your own conclusions. Inevitably, the mirror is a distorting one which makes you see familiar things in a new way. That is how the best insights arise.

As you look into the distorting mirror of the past to examine the present, you will find whatever you want to find. This book does not presume to tell you all the answers: leadership is not so simple that it can be condensed down to a few snappy answers. Instead, it invites you to ask questions, look at your world through a fresh perspective, and to draw your own conclusions.

This book is meant to be a journey of discovery. Hopefully you will enjoy it and, possibly, discover something as well.

THE QUALITIES OF A LEADER

INTRODUCTION

For thousands of years, leaders have got by without having an MBA. If kings and queens needed smart people, they could find plenty of churchmen to provide the brains. And even today, if you look at the planet's top billionaires, they are largely an MBA-free zone. None of the tribal leaders who feature in this book have MBAs, and many of them cannot read.

So there is something more to leadership than having all the skills that a business school can give you. Those skills are important, but they are not enough.

When looking for a leader, tribes do not look at formal qualifications. They look at the person. They do not look at the person's DNA: they are not looking for some innate quality such as charisma and inspiration. They are looking for a simpler set of personal qualities which any of us can acquire with enough effort and determination.

By looking at what makes good tribal leaders and historical leaders, we can find the essence of what makes a good leader today. Leadership in the tribal world is leadership stripped bare: it is the leadership without the corporate life support systems that enable us and imprison us at the same time.

As you take this journey in search of leadership you will make three pleasant discoveries:

■ You do not have to be perfect to be a leader, because no leader is ever perfect.

■ Anyone can learn to lead. There is no mysterious ingredient which you either have or do not have.

■ You do not have to wait until you are CEO before leading: you can show you are a leader at any level of your tribe.

Enjoy your journey in search of the essence of leadership.

CHAPTER 1

THE LEADERSHIP RIDDLE

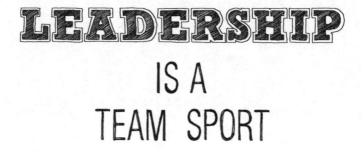

LEADERSHIP
IS A
TEAM SPORT

If you read enough leadership books you will realise that to succeed you need to become an improbable mix of Nelson Mandela, Lord Nelson, Machiavelli, Churchill, Genghis Khan and Mother Teresa all put together. Some bosses think they are already that good: they are normally bosses who are well worth avoiding.

As an experiment, see what happens when you swap Genghis Khan for Mother Teresa. So let Genghis Khan sort out the slums of Calcutta in his own unique way. He would succeed: there would be no slums left. Now imagine Mother Teresa on horseback leading the Mongols on their rampage across Asia. For most people, this does not work.

So it is clear, we cannot succeed by being someone else. We are who we are, and we are not suddenly going to become Churchill or Mandela.

But equally, we cannot succeed by just being ourselves. If we hang around like a teenager in full hormonal angst waiting for the world to recognise our innate genius, humanity and natural leadership talent, we will wait for a very long time.

So we cannot succeed by being someone else and we cannot succeed by just being ourselves. We are doomed.

Or perhaps not. There is one way out of the riddle: be the best of who you are.

"Be the best of who you are" sounds trite, but is not. First, it means focusing on your own unique strengths. Think of various bosses you have had. You may wonder how some of them ever became a boss with their glaring weaknesses. But even my worst bosses had one or two signature strengths which propelled them to the top. Successful leaders are like any successful performer: they build on strength, not on weakness.

Bizarrely, most evaluation and development systems focus on weaknesses or "development opportunities" in the jargon. Olympic athletes do not succeed by focusing on weakness: making weightlifters focus on their synchronised swimming skills would be entertaining, but not effective.

If you want to succeed, work out what you are really good at. Then make sure you find roles where you can play to your strengths. Avoid assignments that focus on your "development opportunities" unless you want to set your career back by years. The way to deal with weaknesses is not to focus on them, but to work around them. Leadership is a team sport, so make sure you have a team that complements your talents: if you are not great at book keeping, or strategy, or customer service, or financial analysis, you can find plenty of people who are.

CHAPTER 2

ARE YOU LEADING?

HOW WILL
YOU
BE REMEMBERED?

Try the following exercise.

Name as many Prime Ministers as you can (or Presidents of your country) since 1945. And name one thing you remember most about them. Here is what I am told by groups when they try this exercise:

Attlee: welfare state
Churchill in peacetime: er . . . not much
Eden: Suez crisis
Macmillan: "You've never had it so good"
Home: Who's he?
Wilson: "White heat of the technology revolution"
   (er . . . which technology was that?)
Heath: Sailing and going into Europe
Wilson again: Pipes, raincoats and the lavender list
Callaghan: Strikes and the three day week
Thatcher: Thatcherism (for better or worse)
Major: er . . . not much
Blair: Iraq
Brown: Financial crisis
Cameron: too early to tell

Few leaders through history get remembered for very much at all. And most of them are not remembered how they would like to be remembered, which is why they are so keen to write their autobiographies. Only Attlee and Thatcher are remotely close to being remembered in a way that they would hope to be remembered. Most Prime Ministers have followed the course of history rather than changing the course of history.

If it is hard for Prime Ministers to be remembered clearly and positively, it is even harder for business leaders to be well remembered. Try naming the leaders of your business for the last 50 years and see how far you get.

So how will you be remembered?

In truth, none of us are likely to be remembered for our great exploits in mastering PowerPoint or closing the month end accounts on time. But we still need to make our mark. If we want to progress on the leadership ladder, we need to stand out from our colleagues. It is not enough to have done well, because everyone else will have done well. You need a distinctive claim to fame. A good claim to fame is where you go above and beyond your normal remit: you take on a challenging project; you lead an initiative which cuts across the organisation; you develop a new idea or a new way of working.

But, as the Prime Minister test shows, it is all too easy to be remembered for the wrong thing.

Just like Prime Ministers, we are likely to be remembered for how we are as much as for what we do. So appearances and behaviour count, especially when in view of senior managers. You can make your mark by being consistently positive, reliable and action focused. These are low hurdles over which most of your colleagues will fall. If you have a presentation to make at a conference, or a proposal to submit, over-invest time in making it superb. Be remembered the right way.

CHAPTER 3

ARE YOU GOOD ENOUGH TO LEAD?

I was walking through the bush when a randy ostrich decided to attack: we were crossing his territory. There are many distinguished ways of dying in the bush. Being eaten by crocodiles or lions at least gives your family a good story to remember you by. But being disembowelled by a randy ostrich means you are as likely to die of shame as you are from the disembowelment.

Unfortunately, ostriches are one of the fastest animals on land. They can reach 70 kilometres an hour, which would get them a speeding ticket in London. Fortunately, I was faster than my guides. You do not need to outrun an ostrich, you need to outrun your peers.

The same is true of the leadership race. You do not need to be the best leader on the planet. No leader gets ticks in all the boxes: even the best leaders have their faults. And this does not matter. You simply need to be better than your colleagues in a relevant way. The trick is to know what the "relevant way" is for your desired role. This is where things become tricky: the rules of survival and success change at each level of the firm:

■ When you start out on the leadership race, the expectations at least are clear. New and aspiring leaders may not have much power or control, but at least they have clarity about what they must do. To succeed, you have to show that you have mastered your trade, be it trading, teaching or technology.

■ In the next stage of the leadership race, you find all the rules change. It is no longer about being the best technician. Leadership is about getting things done through other people: managing people becomes essential. Many aspiring leaders do not realise that the rules of the game have changed and their career is effectively disembowelled. They go nowhere very fast.

■ As you rise to more senior positions, the rules of survival and success change again. Managing people well is not enough. You have to manage the organisation and its politics: making alliances, doing deals, building trust, aligning agendas.

■ Once you finally achieve top leadership, things become easier: your authority and responsibility is more in balance and any ambiguity is entirely of your own making. Whisper it quietly, but leading from the top is easier than leading from the middle. Top leaders often fail because they do not know how to handle their new-found freedom: they are either too timid or too bold.

At evaluation time, ignore the formal evaluation systems, which are little more than school reports for grown ups. Ask yourself what you need to be doing to perform better than your peers in a way that is relevant to bosses at the top of the organisation.

CHAPTER 4

THE PERFECT LEADER

THE SAME PERSON
IN DIFFERENT CONTEXTS
COULD BE A

HERO

OR A

ZERO

No leader in history has been perfect. You do not need to be perfect either, because perfection does not exist in leadership. Searching for perfection is like searching for smoke signals in the fog: it is an exercise in futility. By way of illustration, try the next two exercises.

First, imagine you are on safari. Look at all the animals and decide which one is the perfect predator. Some people say it is the lion because the lion is the king of the jungle: but lions do not live in jungles. Some favour the elephant because all animals give way to the elephant at a watering hole. Others favour cheetahs for their speed, hippos for their aggression and crocodiles for their menace.

This is an argument which could go round in circles. So perhaps we should compromise by creating the perfect predator out of all the animals we have seen. Now we land up with a predator with the jaws of a crocodile, ears of an elephant, neck of a giraffe, wings of an eagle, hide of a rhino, legs of a cheetah and the tail of a scorpion. The beast will promptly die under the weight of its own improbability.

Returning to Planet Business, try another exercise: design the perfect leader. We can start with what the experts say a perfect leader should look like. Putting together all the theories, the perfect leader looks like this:

- Visionary and detailed
- Controlling and empowering
- People focused and task focused
- Ambitious and humble
- Strategic and operational
- Risk taking and reliable

The perfect leader is like the perfect predator: it cannot exist.

If perfection does not make a leader, what does? The answer is provided by another animal: a reindeer. In the Arctic, reindeer migrate from the mountains to the sea at the end of each harsh winter. They appear to survive on nothing, scratching at the odd piece of exposed rock with lichen on it. So now you have to decide whether the reindeer or the lion is the perfect beast. The answer is that both are perfect . . . for their environment. The reindeer would not last long in the Maasai Mara and a lion in the Arctic would not be a happy lion.

And the same goes with leaders: there are only leaders who fit and leaders who do not fit. Churchill is the classic example. Before the war he was something of a misfit. In the war he became the great British hero. When he became Prime Minister again after the war, he is memorable for more or less nothing. The same person in different contexts could be a hero or a zero: the person did not change, the context changed.

As leaders, we have to find the context in which we can best flourish.

CHAPTER 5

THE LEADER AS A ROLE MODEL

Think back about the various bosses you have had. Try to recall two things about each one:

1. how well they performed against their annual objective
2. what they were like as a boss and as a person

The chances are that you can remember much more about what they were like than about how they performed. And this is just how you will be remembered as well.

You will be remembered for both the small things and the big things. For instance, we were walking through the bush with a tribal elder and two young warriors. The young warriors were like teenagers anywhere: playing about and not really focusing on the task in hand which was to patrol the tribal boundary. As we walked, the elder often stopped to pick up a bit of litter while the young warriors kept on fooling around. The elder said nothing. After a few hours the young warriors stopped fooling around and started following the leader. Eventually, one of them spotted a piece of litter and picked it up himself. The elder allowed himself a quiet smile. The day's lesson had been a success, without him having to say anything or having any argument.

As a leader, how you behave determines how your team will react. If you are a miserable Machiavellian miser, do not expect your team to be open, generous and happy.

Your team will pick up your style from both small and big moments of truth. Small moments of truth happen all the time:

■ How often do you say thank you?
■ What is your ratio of giving praise to criticising and questioning?
■ Did you show any personal interest in any of your staff today?

The bigger moments of truth are rarer: in practice, you need to be prepared for them so that you can react the way you want to, rather than producing a reaction under stress. Compare how you dealt with each of the following moments of truth in the past with how you want to deal with them next time around:

■ crisis of under-performance or missed deadlines
■ dispute with another department
■ a stroppy boss, colleague or customer

As ever, you will be remembered as much for how you dealt with the problem as with the final outcome. To test yourself on your style, create a series of Mr Men (or their female equivalents): Mr Angry, Mr Bored, Mr Crazy, Mr Diligent, Mr Energetic, Mr Fib and so on. At the start of each day decided which character you want to be; at the end, see which one you were and figure out why. Most leaders think they are positive role models; most followers think otherwise. Be honest in your self-assessment and you will find that you force yourself into becoming a positive role model.

You will be remembered as much for how you are as for what you do.

CHAPTER 6

THE LEADER'S VALUES

Everyone in the village said the same thing. The women, the men, the children and the elders all said that what they most wanted to see in a good leader was courage, contribution and responsibility. I half expected that their huts would have little brass plaques saying "courage, contribution, responsibility". Or perhaps they would have one of those motivational posters of people rowing up a mountain to make the same point. And then there would be the video from the chief. But the village was dirt poor. They had no electricity or water, let alone motivational posters and brass plaques.

The unanimity of the village was impressive. But I still felt a bit cynical about this corporate-style spouting of the village values. If in doubt, watch the feet, not the mouth. People's actions do not lie.

I was on patrol with a couple of warriors when suddenly, out of the bush, a pack of hyenas came charging straight at us. I did what any sensible coward would do. I hid behind the warriors: they would get killed first and I could run away. The warriors then laughed in the face of imminent death. This struck me as one reason they were warriors and I was not.

The cause of their laughter became clear a moment later. Out of the same piece of bush came a small child with an even smaller stick chasing the hyenas. That was a moment of madness born of years, of generations, of cultural indoctrination. The child had been protecting the entire wealth of the village: its goats. And the child knew it had to protect the goats at all costs. Even the hyenas knew they had met their match.

Suddenly, the values came to life. The child had shown much more courage than I had. Its contribution in protecting the wealth of the village was beyond doubt. And it took responsibility: the child did not run back to the village to convene an emergency plenary session of the hyena sub-committee of the wildlife management task force to decide what to do. The child picked up a stick and attacked.

Today's leaders do not need physical courage. But they do need courage to take unpopular decisions and to lead people where they would not have gone by themselves. And the scandals over executive pay and bankers' bonuses shine a light on the need to balance contribution more evenly with reward: are our leaders in it for the money, or for what they can contribute?

And finally, responsibility: all leaders find it easy to take responsibility for success. Few have the courage to take responsibility for setbacks. But until the leader takes responsibility for setbacks, it is hard for the firm to move on.

There are many other values which a leader can adopt. Courage, contribution and responsibility are good for some tribes, not so relevant for others. But it does not matter what the formal values statement says. Formal values statements are a good way of keeping superannuated executives harmlessly occupied, and give a nice speech for the CEO to deliver. But the carefully nuanced words make little difference. The only way the values come to life is when the leader lives those values.

What are the values you want to live by, and how do you show them at work?

CHAPTER 7

COURAGE AND LEADERSHIP

Throughout history, leaders have been expected to be brave. Kings were meant to lead their troops into battle, rather than sitting in a bunker issuing commands by secure telephone. Shakespeare's Henry V is heroic because he shares the same risks as his soldiers and is an example to all who follow him.

So what has courage got to do with leadership today? It does not take great courage to close the month-end accounts. Physical bravery does not appear on the must-have list of qualities for the CEO of your firm.

But you cannot be a good leader without courage. Both emerging and established leaders need courage.

Emerging leaders

The emerging leader needs courage to grow and learn. If you never fail, you have never tried hard enough. This lesson was taught to me in ski school. We were told to "bend zee knees" and do our snow plough turns. Meanwhile, there was a joker who was always trying out the fancy professional turns and kept on falling over. How we laughed at him. By the end of the week we were not laughing any more. He was on the advanced slopes having mastered the fancy turns and we were still doing snow plough turns on the easy routes. He had courage to learn, push himself and fail: we stayed in our comfort zone.

In business we have to face our demons. We have to learn to speak in public, deal with conflict, resolve crises, stand up for our interests, deal with difficult bosses and colleagues. If we do not do these things, we will never lead.

Established leaders

Henry Kissinger, the US Secretary of State during the Vietnam war, defined leadership as "Taking people where they would not have got by themselves". Many leaders fail this test: they simply administer a legacy which they inherited. Taking people where they would not have gone by themselves takes moral courage, not least of all because there is a real risk of failure. Followers will inevitably have their doubts and are ready to point the finger of blame when things go wrong. Failure is always lonely. Until leaders are able to take difficult, and often unpopular, decisions, they are not leading. Leadership always takes courage.

CHAPTER 8

LEARNING
COURAGE

Courage appears to be one of those qualities, like charisma, charm and beauty, that you either have or don't have. Fortunately, this is not true. Courage can be learned in the same way that most of the skills and qualities of a leader can be learned. You do not have to be born a leader: you have to work at it.

Bill, the local fire chief, was astonished and offended when asked about the bravery of his firemen. "I never want my firemen being brave. I want them to be effective," was his tart response to the idea of bravery. And yet to outsiders, firemen are brave: going into smoke-filled buildings with unknown hazards, low visibility and worse is not everyone's idea of a normal day in the office.

How do firemen acquire the bravery to do things that most of us would not do?

They learn courage incrementally. They start with simple tasks and slowly move on to more and more challenging tasks. And then they keep on repeating the most challenging tasks time and time again. Slowly, the unfamiliar becomes familiar and the exceptional becomes routine. With practice, even bravery becomes so routine that they do not see it that way: they see it as a natural part of their job.

And so it is with leadership and courage. If you try to be too brave you will fail: all the dangers, demons and risks will loom large. If you have never spoken in public before, do not make your first attempt a speech in front of the entire firm. Build up incrementally: get used to talking at meetings and small groups, then take on larger roles in larger groups. Eventually, addressing the entire firm will seem like a simple and routine task.

Courage can be learned when you make the exceptional become the routine.

CHAPTER 9

RESPONSIBLE
LEADERSHIP

Harry S. Truman, the US President, famously had a sign on his desk saying "the buck stops here". He was right. The buck always stops with the leader. You can and should delegate tasks. You should also delegate some of your authority so that people can complete their tasks. But you can never delegate away your responsibility.

But what is the leader really responsible for? I found the answer in the middle of the open steppe in Mongolia. I was with the sports superstar of Mongolia: Choidog. In a horse-crazy country, he was their champion horse trainer. A nadaam, or festival, was being held to honour his lifetime of achievement. There was wrestling, eating, drinking and, of course, a horse race. Two hundred horses set off across the steppe: it was like seeing the Mongol hordes emerging out of nowhere.

The race had been rigged. Choidog's horse was meant to win the valuable prize of the motorbike. Sure enough, his horse took the lead. But then disaster struck: the saddle came off the horse. So the 12-year-old jockey got off the horse, put the saddle back on and then rode like the wind towards the finish line. He very nearly managed to win. But very nearly does not win a prize.

So Choidog's big day was ruined and he did not get a motorbike. And his reaction?

"It was my fault," he said, with a rueful smile on his face. "I should have checked the saddle myself. And it was my fault that the jockey did not know that he was meant to let the saddle fall off and to continue bare back. I should have trained him better."

By taking responsibility for failure, Choidog avoided the common corporate reaction to setbacks: the blame game, denial, avoidance and politics as everyone tries to dodge the bullet.

But Choidog was being responsible for far more than the outcome. He had every right to feel frustrated, annoyed, angry or depressed. Instead, he enjoyed the rest of the day with visiting friends, family and dignitaries. He had taken responsibility for his own feelings. He chose to enjoy the day rather than dwell on the setback.

All the time we can choose how we feel: we can feel good or bad about what is happening around us. That is our choice: it is not a requirement of the job. There is an old adage about what makes a good Prime Minister: it is better to have a PM with a first class temperament than a first class mind. The same is true of all leaders. You can always find smart people to do the intellectual heavy lifting, but you cannot delegate away your temperament and style. No one wants moody, sulking, angry, cynical and frustrated leaders. Like Choidog, you can choose how you feel. You can focus on the bad things and setbacks in life, or you can focus on the good things and find the positives.

If you can master the elusive art of being responsible for your own feelings, you cannot only lead better, you can live better.

CHAPTER 10

WEAR THE MASK

WHAT IS
THE MASK
YOU WANT
TO PRESENT
TO THE
REST OF
THE
WORLD?

All leaders have to learn to wear the mask of leadership. As followers, we want to follow leaders we respect and admire, even if occasionally we have to follow leaders who fall short. To be a leader that followers want to follow, we have to live up to their expectations. We have to be the best of who we are and we have to adapt our style to our role.

In traditional societies, wearing the mask is not a metaphor: it is reality, as I discovered in a shabby town in Papua New Guinea. I fell in with some dangerous looking locals: they were dressed in second-hand clothes from the west. One sported a T-shirt advertising the Tijuana Rock Festival 1992, with a picture of a joint on it. A day later, we reached the village where these locals lived. The Tijuana rock festival person changed into his formal gear: grass skirt, body paint and an immense headdress made from bird of paradise feathers. It was Chief John in all his finery. He transformed himself from another local layabout into a regal chief.

This was not simply a matter of dress for success: you will certainly make an impression in the office if you come in wearing a grass skirt, body paint and not much more. He not only changed his dress, he changed his style. He stood straighter; his voice dropped; he spoke more slowly and more deliberately; he quit joking and fooling around.

Modern leaders may not have headdresses, but they still learn to wear the mask. Tony Blair was forced to learn the lesson from civil servants who all addressed him as "Prime Minister". He recalled it was an out-of-body experience, as he kept on wondering who they were talking about. It was a constant reminder that he was more than just "Tony", and more was expected from him.

As David, the CEO of a recruitment company, put it: "I still get angry and bored or frustrated but I have learned not to show it. If a crisis or an argument is looming, I just put on the mask of leadership. Don't get dragged in. Lead by example. If you get angry, you give permission for others to get angry. Then you go nowhere. You have to behave how you want others to behave."

What is the mask you want to present to the rest of the world? What you think and feel behind the mask is for you alone: let the world react to the mask.

CHAPTER 11

POPULARITY VERSUS RESPECT

BUILD RESPECT, NOT POPULARITY

People like to be liked. And we can now count our friends on Facebook and see how popular we are: competitive social approval is here to stay.

As most leaders are also human beings, it is natural that leaders want to be liked. Machiavelli, writing in 1512, observed this and saw the dangers of succumbing to Facebook-style popularity. He saw the essential weakness in seeking to be liked: people are fickle in what and who they like, and so courting popularity is a dead end. You seek popularity by giving one concession, and that simply sets up the expectation of more concessions. You remain as popular as you are weak, and your popularity will be eclipsed by any other leader who is more generous than you are.

Machiavelli advised that "it is better to be feared than it is to be liked". He then went on to suggest that a few token executions would keep everyone in order and prevent chaos breaking out. Be cruel to be kind. Leaders today may not execute staff, but they often fire a few staff and put their own team in place. It has the same effect as the executions: it allows leaders to take control. But a fear-based work place is one where you can ensure compliance but you cannot generate commitment. Compliance achieves minimum effort to avoid sanctions:

only through commitment can you achieve out-standing efforts and results.

But the true currency of leadership is neither popularity nor fear. It is respect. No one wants to work for a leader they do not respect. Most of us are happy to work for a leader we respect. Respect is different from popularity, as shown below:

	Popularity	Respect
Underperformance	Avoid issue until too late: annual evaluation	Deal with issue early and positively: find a way forward
Workloads	Set easy targets	Set stretching targets
Conflict of priorities	Avoid issue, concede, don't fight	Be assertive , find a win win.
Decisions	Take the easy way forward	Do what's right

Seeking popularity achieves nothing other than an easy life in the short term. The effective leader will build respect, not popularity.

CHAPTER 12

BE POSITIVE

BE POSITIVE

Late 1940 was a bad time. Britain stood on the edge of a continent which was armed and hostile. Invasion, and probable defeat, seemed imminent. There were plenty of people who were quietly hoping to do a deal with the forces of darkness. And many more felt less than confident about the future. So did Churchill commission some focus groups and echo what people were thinking to build his popularity as a new Prime Minister?

Churchill did not follow focus groups and consensus: he positively led. Most of his great speeches and phrases come from those dark days:

- "I have nothing to offer but blood sweat and tears . . ."
- "This was their finest hour . . ."
- "We will fight them on the beaches . . . we will never surrender"
- "Never . . . have so many owed so much to so few"

You never heard Churchill say:

- "We are in real trouble"
- "It's not my fault, I sent the email to finance last week"

■ "Let's call in some consultants to produce a report"

Being positive is not about saying "have a nice day" behind clenched teeth while meaning "please just drop dead". A positive leader follows some consistent principles that anyone can learn:

■ Focus on the end outcome. Look at where you want to get to. In an argument, do you want to win the intellectual argument and moral high ground, thereby creating an enemy for life? Or do you want to make a friend and find a way forward? Your choice.

■ Drive to action. In the middle of a crisis everything may seem out of control. The positive leader will not worry about what cannot be controlled: that simply leads to stress and anxiety. The effective leader will focus on what can be controlled and will act on that, however small it may be: offering blood, sweat and tears was all Churchill could do, so he did it.

■ Find the positives: avoid the blame game, navel gazing and analysing the past. Driving to the future by looking in the rear mirror normally results in a crash. Even in the worst situations there will be some positives: focus on those.

■ Act the part. If you are not enthusiastic, no one else will be enthusiastic for you. You will find your team mirrors your style: they will be as open, defensive, positive or as miserable as you are.

These behaviours do not come naturally to many of us. But with practice they become second nature, because they work.

CHAPTER 13

INSPIRATION
AND CHARISMA

Many of the great leaders down the ages have been inspirational and charismatic figures. This is a disaster for the modern leader. They have set the bar too high and in the wrong place for any of us as leaders. Most of us cannot hope to be as inspirational as Martin Luther King, or Henry V urging our team "once more unto the breach" to finish the project on time.

Although history teaches us that there have been many inspirational and charismatic leaders, history also teaches us that there are many more leaders who are not inspirational and charismatic. Most tribal leaders I worked with were not inspirational or charismatic, although they were very good at leading their tribes. In the same way, most business leaders I have worked with can lead their business tribe, often very well, with a complete lack of charisma

Fortunately, there is an alternative to being inspirational and charismatic. This is good news for most us: we do not have to rely on inheriting the right genes or wait for medical science to create a charisma transplant service.

The alternative to charisma is professionalism. The best leaders in modern and ancient tribes were all devastatingly effective in their trade. Most of them had learned their trade over decades: the tribal leaders had grown up learning to lead, the business leaders had survived the management marathon.

Of course, professionalism is one vague word that can be used to describe another vague word: leadership. For leaders, professionalism encompasses a wide range of craft skills which anyone can learn. These skills include: communicating, motivating, clear thinking, making decisions, monitoring and all the other activities that leaders have to learn. Critically, they have to learn them in context: the way an investment banker makes a decision is completely different from the way that a civil servant makes a decision. Putting a civil servant in charge of an investment bank, or an investment banker in charge of the civil service, is asking for trouble.

Once leaders become devastatingly effective at the craft skills of communicating, motivating and clear thinking a curious thing happens. Followers start to think that the leader is inspirational and charismatic.

The good news for all of us is that charisma and inspiration are the exception, not the rule, for leaders. Instead, if we focus on becoming ever more professional and effective in our core craft skills, we can succeed and we may even start to be seen as inspirational and charismatic.

CHAPTER 14

BE AMBITIOUS AND UNREASONABLE

If Alexander the Great had been reasonable, he would have realised that he could only rule his tinpot state on the far edge of Greek civilisation. Alexander the Great was not reasonable. He conquered the whole of the known world, and a bit beyond, by the age of 30. That is why he became Alexander the Great, unlike his obscure cousin Alexander the Reasonable.

Being reasonable is a disaster for leaders. There are always reasons why the project will be late, why costs must go up, why we must cut our prices, why budget will be missed. When you accept excuses, you accept failure. Good leaders are ambitious and unreasonable.

Ambition is not just personal ambition, although that is needed if you are to survive the management marathon. Leaders are always ambitious for the organisations they lead as well. Ambition means having the courage to chase challenging goals that force the firm into business not as usual: force people out of their comfort zone and discover new ways of doing things.

Being ambitious is inherently unreasonable: you are setting goals that are not easy to achieve. But if you want to conquer the business world, or drive your organisation forward, you have to be unreasonable. Reasonable managers accept all the reasons why something cannot be achieved. I repeat: when you accept excuses, you accept failure.

Most of the great businesses today were not created by reasonable people. Ryanair was insane to take on the might of British Airways; Google had no chance against the power of Lycos, MSN, Excite and AOL; Dyson could never win against Hoover. If Michael O'Leary, Larry Page, Sergey Brin and James Dyson had listened to reason, they would have given up before they started. Other reasonable people have had brilliant ideas, but we have never heard of them because they listened to all the reasons why they could not succeed.

There is an art form to being unreasonable as a leader. It is not about shouting at people, arguing and demeaning colleagues. If you ask for the moon, you have to help people get there. In practice that means:

- Be unreasonable about the goal and stick to it
- Be flexible about the means: don't second guess your team

■ Support your team all the way: money and
  political support
■ Don't be deflected by setbacks

To lead is to live beyond the comfort zone. The
art of leadership is helping others stretch themselves, develop and live outside their comfort zone
as well.

CHAPTER 15

EARNING
RESPECT

The old man sat in the dusty village square and started off: "The problem with young people today is respect. . . ." You can travel beyond Timbuktu into the wilder parts of Mali and find old people are the same everywhere: demanding respect from the young for their elders and betters.

And then the old man sprang a surprise:

"Young people need to learn to respect themselves: if they can achieve something, be good at something, contribute something then they will learn to respect themselves. Only when people respect themselves are they able to respect anyone else. They might even start respecting their elders . . . if we deserve it." The old man had unwrapped another nugget of leadership insight and presented it to me.

However old or young you are, respect has to be earned. For many leaders, respect is elusive. Respect appears to come with your title. When you first become a big boss you will find that suddenly everyone thinks your jokes are hilarious, your insights are profound and your taste in everything from music to wine is impeccable. This will come as some surprise since you probably have spent many years having people respond in stony silence to your jokes, ripping apart your brightest ideas and mocking your taste in everything. Leadership has changed everything.

As a leader, it is very easy to start believing what people say to your face. But you can be sure that behind your back they are making a much more even-handed appraisal of your performance, jokes, ideas and taste.

Title will get you superficial respect, but real respect always has to be earned, however senior you become.

Think for a moment about leaders you have respected, and why you respected them. Most executives identify some combination of the following in leaders they have respected:

- Show you care for your team and your colleagues
- Be positive, especially when times are tough
- Be clear and consistent in your expectations
- Have difficult conversations where needed, but make them positive
- Always deliver on all your commitments, so take care about what you promise

As with much in leadership, this is not rocket science. But most leaders struggle to maintain these standards. If you can do all these things well, you will not only earn respect, you will stand out from most of your peers.

CHAPTER 16

WORK—LIFE BALANCE

HOW OFTEN HAVE
YOU HEARD A

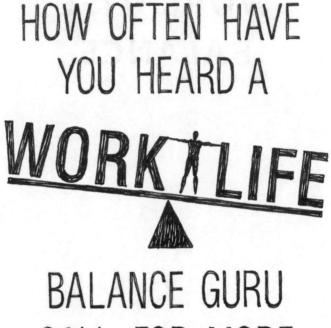

BALANCE GURU
CALL FOR MORE
WORK?

How many leaders or other top professionals have you met who hate their job and are cynical about what they do? Such people may exist, but mostly people vote with their feet. If they dislike something, they move. Most leaders may ritually grumble about hard work or jet lag, but that is mainly to boast about how hard they work and how far they travel. In practice, most leaders and most top professionals are addicted to what they do. CEOs want to give up as rarely as top footballers or musicians want to retire.

Throughout history, top leaders have tended towards 24/7 working. This is true in every traditional society, for the simple reason that tribes do not do privacy. The leader is constantly visible, constantly on display and constantly on call. And they love it: it is not just a job, it is a life.

It can also be seriously hard work. Herding reindeer sounds a gentle task. Except that 800 reindeer all have (small) minds of their own and are likely to scatter if given half a chance for five minutes. And they keep moving for up to one week at a time during the migration. So to herd the reindeer you have to keep going for a week: the most sleep you will get is for a few minutes a time on the back of a snowmobile as the temperature falls to −40 centigrade. It is a job you do for love, not money.

In the business world there is much talk about the work–life balance. How often have you heard a work–life balance guru call for more work? "Work–life balance" is a euphemism for working less. We are already the idlest generation in history: we work fewer hours for fewer weeks a year for fewer years than any generation in the past. We should celebrate our luck.

But if we want to get to the top and stay there, we need to make some choices. There is no short cut to leadership on a four hour week.

There is no point in aspiring to leadership unless you enjoy it. You only excel at what you enjoy. Only when you truly enjoy what you do will you find the stamina to keep going year after year, to remain positive, to overcome all the crises and conflicts which erupt on your journey.

For leaders, the work–life balance discussion is the wrong discussion. The right discussion is "what do you most enjoy doing and what do you want to do?" If you want to reduce your working time, that is probably a sign that either you have a very compelling domestic life, or that you are not totally satisfied with your work life.

To succeed, you have to find the context in which you can thrive. Enjoyment is not the result of success: it is a requirement for success.

CHAPTER 17

LUCKY LEADERS

LUCK

PREPARATION PERSISTENCE PRACTICE PRACTICE PREPARATION PERSISTENCE PREPARATION PERSISTENCE PREPARATION PRACTICE PERSISTENCE PREPARATION PERSISTENCE PERSISTENCE PREPARATION PRACTICE

is not luck at all

Napoleon famously preferred generals who were lucky. Until he met Wellington. But are leaders lucky? Most leaders are very ambiguous and unhelpful on the matter of luck. If you ask them, their standard response will be: "I have been very lucky, but of course I made most of my luck." So was that luck or not? It clarifies more or less nothing.

Arnold Palmer, the golfing legend, shed some light on the matter when he declared, "The harder I practise, the luckier I get." In other words, a putt with a 20% chance of success, becomes a 40% chance with practice. The 40% chance becomes a 60% chance and the 60% chance becomes an 80% chance. In other words, luck is not luck at all.

Richard Wiseman, a professor at Hertfordshire University, decided to study luck. He found luck boiled down to three things:

- Practice
- Preparation
- Persistence

We have already looked at practice. Preparation is about knowing what you are looking for. You will not see what you are not looking for.

Persistence is what it says: keep going. Wiseman found one woman who was incredibly lucky. She was always winning lotteries and competitions. She won free cars, free holidays and free money. She helped herself by entering over 250 competitions a week. In the course of doing so, she became expert at giving competition judges what they wanted. Practice and persistence go hand in hand.

Wiseman made one further, critical, discovery about lucky people. Lucky people are not actually luckier than most other people. They simply think they are lucky.

To see how lucky you are, try this exercise. First, think of all the bad things that have happened today: delays on the way to work, annoying habits of colleagues, not getting replies to emails, stupid forms you have to fill in, your tax return. So are you lucky?

Now re-run the movie of your day and focus on all the good fortune you have enjoyed. You woke up in a warm bed; you have access to hot and cold running water; you have public or private transport; you have a job: simply by being born a human in an affluent country in the current era you have hit the jackpot in life's lottery. So are you lucky?

You are as lucky as you want to feel. And as a leader, you make your own luck.

THE SKILLS OF THE LEADER

INTRODUCTION

It is not enough to have the right personal qualities to succeed as a leader. A good leader is also a skilled leader.

Most leadership research asks leaders what makes great leaders. That is an exercise in flattery which achieves little beyond soothing the outsized egos of a few CEOs. But for real insight you need a fresh perspective. In this case, the perspective came from interviewing not just the leaders, but their followers as well. What the leaders thought of themselves and what their followers thought were often very different, and not to the credit of the leader.

The results from thousands of followers around the world are fairly consistent. There are five consistent answers. Followers want a leader who:

- Has a clear vision
- Can motivate people
- Is decisive
- Handles crises well
- Has honesty and integrity

Apart from honesty and integrity, these are all skills that anyone can learn. And it is worth noting what is not there: charisma and inspiration do not make the cut. That is just as well. Most leaders, and most of us, are not naturally charismatic. You cannot train charisma and medical science has not yet invented the charisma transplant service.

This section looks at the core skills all leaders must learn, and how you can learn them in practice.

CHAPTER 18

TECHNICAL SKILLS VERSUS PEOPLE SKILLS

technical skills
are a

DEAD
END

for leaders

It's easy to make things complicated, and much harder to make them simple. Leadership can be as complicated and as sophisticated as you want it to be. But if you strip away the noise, the essence of leadership is simple: it's about people.

In the highlands of Papua New Guinea, sophistication is a luxury they cannot afford. To survive, they have to keep things simple. When we finally arrived at the village, the chief had to make a decision: should we be allowed to stay?

He could have made the decision himself, and in his mind he had made the decision. But a decision which is not accepted is not a decision: it is a hope.

So he called a meeting of everyone in the village. He was offered the only chair the village possessed. We sat on the only bench behind the only table in the village. Everyone else sat on a mud track which was the only road in the village.

After a couple of hours, it was good news for us and bad news for the pig. There would be a welcome feast and the pig would be the feast. For the chief, leadership was not something you did from the safety of a desk. As John le Carre wrote in *Tinker Tailor Soldier Spy* "a desk is a dangerous place from which to view the world". To lead people where they would not go by themselves you have to be with the people.

To say that leadership is about people is possibly trite, but it has profound implications for anyone who wants to lead. Most people when they start out their career learn some craft skills – which might be financial analysis, accounting, law, teaching, using PowerPoint – as needed in each career. If they master the craft, they may well be promoted. And that is where the problems start.

The newly-promoted leader is promoted for technical skills, and will naturally want to focus on reinforcing those skills: technical excellence is the success formula that they have learned gets them promotion. But technical skills are a dead end for leaders.

The job of the leader is not to be the best technician in the team, just as the job of the football manager is not to be the best player on the pitch. The manager is not meant to make every tackle and pass and score every goal. The manager is there to make sure the right team is in place, to motivate them, train them, give them the right support, direct them and move them on when needed. In other words, leadership is about people skills, not technical skills. So the leader has to learn a completely new success formula if they are to survive in their new role.

The journey to leadership is full of bear traps and dead ends. Building technical skills is the biggest dead end of all. It is vital for early success, but goes nowhere in the longer term. Leaders learn to leave the technical skills path and start exploring the path of people skills.

CHAPTER 19

ABILITY TO MOTIVATE OTHERS

FEAR

DRIVES
COMPLIANCE
BUT
IT
DOES
NOT
DRIVE
PERFORMANCE

Motivational theory doesn't crop up much when you are living in a mud hut. Mostly, people are more concerned about whether the rains will come and the crops will grow. Despite this lack of theory, or perhaps because of it, there is not much of a problem motivating people to work hard, long and with commitment.

Tribes apply the theory of motivation without knowing it. Many business leaders know the theory, but do not apply it.

The ability to motivate people is one of the top expectations that followers have of their leaders. Leaders tend to rate their motivational ability highly; followers consistently score leaders lowest on their ability to motivate. And it is a truism that most people do not leave their firm: they leave their boss.

Maslow observed that we are all needs junkies: once we have fulfilled one need, we move on to the next one. Here is his pyramid of needs:

1. Physiological needs: food, water
2. Safety and security
3. Sense of belonging
4. Recognition
5. Leave a legacy

Here is how his theory works in both the tribal and business worlds:

1. *Physiological needs:* food, water (having a job). To this day, many tribes struggle with the reality of avoiding starvation. In the modern world, if you do not have a job, any job can suddenly seem attractive to pay the rent.

2. *Safety and security.* Fear is a great way of building compliance: many tribes still live in fear of their neighbours. You never know when a raiding party might appear. And if you live in Somalia, which has not had a functioning government for years, then fear will make you appreciate any warlord or religious cult who can guarantee your safety. In the business world, fear drives compliance but it does not drive performance. Performance requires extra effort: that requires a higher level of motivation.

3. *Sense of belonging.* Tribal initiation rites are gruesome, but help create deep bonds between members of the tribe. In Mongolia, nomads were astonished to hear that we pay people to help us move house in London: "That's what friends are for," they said, shocked. Today's staff often hop between firms. There is little

sense of commitment to the community. Effective leaders minimise this by creating a sense of belonging. Show that the team is engaged in meaningful work with a worthwhile goal. Create an ésprit de corps so that everyone is proud to belong: top firms do this. Anyone who has worked for McKinsey, Goldman Sachs or Procter & Gamble is always proud of the fact, long after they have left the firm.

4. *Recognition.* Tribes do not pay well, but they recognise well. Good leaders do the same thing. Many high-performing and long-surviving organisations have modest pay: think of the armed services, churches and the voluntary sector. Recognition is not pay: it is about making sure each individual is valued and recognised for what they do. Peer group pressure and peer group respect are powerful motivators. We judge ourselves relative to our peers. We want to look good in front of them and want to avoid failing them. Recognition is a powerful tool for leaders. Pay and bonus is remarkably ineffective as an incentive scheme. It encourages game playing and divisiveness between departments. And the incentive lasts for as long as it takes for the payment to clear the banking system.

5. *Leave a legacy.* In the tribal world, leaving a legacy means survival of the tribe. Modern leaders often seek to leave a legacy through sponsoring a charity or foundation, or going into committee- and commission-land in search of a knighthood. The tribal legacy is about the community; the modern leader's legacy is often about personal vanity. It shows, and it corrodes morale within the firm.

Finally, there is one key motivation which all leaders can use. Followers who rated their boss highly on motivation consistently answered positively to the statement: "my boss cares about me and my career personally" (agree/disagree). Tribal leaders found it hard to believe that anyone might not be interested personally in each member of their tribe. But this is a low hurdle over which many leaders fall. Invest enough time to show that you really do care about each member of your team and you will stand out against many of your peers, and you may even have a highly-motivated team.

CHAPTER 20

CREATING A VISION

A VISION

IS A STORY IN

THREE PARTS

Firms are meant to have visions and leaders are meant to be visionary. History tells us that visions and visionaries are very dangerous indeed. For every leader who marches you to the Promised Land, there is another that marches you straight back into the desert. You don't know whether a vision is good or bad until it is far too late. And most of the great despots, megalomaniacs and dictators of history have had grand visions, which normally meant conquering the world. That is good or bad depending which side you are on. Alexander is known as Alexander the Great in the Western tradition and Alexander the Barbarian in the Persian tradition: he destroyed their ancient civilisation.

Most of us cannot and will not be great visionaries. We are not going to be like Martin Luther King and announce, "I have a dream . . .". If you dream in the office, you are well advised not to stand on your desk and tell the office, "I have a dream . . .".

And yet, visions are important. They give a sense of direction, purpose, meaning and focus. They are a rallying point for all the different tribes within the firm. So how can a practising leader deal with the vision thing?

Fortunately, a vision is very simple. A vision is a story in three parts:

- This is where we are
- This is where we are going
- This is how we are going to get there.

It does not matter if you are leading a team, a tribe, a firm or a nation: anyone can craft a story which is relevant for the group that they are leading.

And if you want to make your vision inspirational and motivational, then you need add one more element to your vision:

- This is your very important role in helping us achieve the vision.

In other words, make the vision personal and practical. If your vision is to delight your customers, then you can make that very relevant to everyone from the janitor upwards: what sort of customer will be delighted by a dirty washroom? Even the janitor has a vital role to play in making your vision of excellence and customer service come true.

What's your vision for your team?

CHAPTER 21

DECISION MAKING

No one likes to follow an indecisive leader who has no sense of direction and is always changing their mind. It leads to uncertainty, delay, conflict and waste of effort. Leaders must be decisive.

Decision making has never been easy: the ancients relied on soothsayers and oracles to help them make decisions. King Croesus famously asked what would happen if he attacked the Persian Empire. The Oracle at Delphi told him that a great empire would fall. Delighted, Croesus assaulted the Persians and discovered the Oracle was right. But it was not the Persian Empire which fell; it was his own.

To see what decision making is like without the corporate overhead of committees, task forces, consultants and other latter day soothsayers with their chicken bones and PowerPoint, it makes sense to travel back into the bush. All the elders were gathered around a fire. A goat was having its throat slit for a feast. Martha was with the elders. She had kissed her husband goodbye one morning in Nairobi, but he never came back: he had been killed in a mugging. So Martha was left with a mortgage, two kids, no insurance and no income.

So she took the initiative. She asked the local tribe if she could set up a small embroidery business with them. She and the elders talked about it for a day and a night. The conversation revolved around three questions:

- Does this fit with where we are going (our vision)? In this case it did: they wanted to move away from pure subsistence farming, and this was a chance to build something new.
- Does it fit with our values? This was tough: the tribe was acutely conscious that bringing money in could lead to divisiveness, envy and competition. They had to find a way of making sure that everyone would benefit: building a school from any profit was the preferred solution.
- How will it work? There were simple questions like: where would Martha live and work? Who would help her? Would she be safe?

When a leader is faced with a tight decision, these are good questions to ask. The financial case is also important. But it is surprising how often spreadsheets are able to produce the answer the leader wants by the simple expedient of plugging in the right assumptions.

In both corporate and tribal worlds, good decision making is not just about the decision. A good process requires fair process: even if someone does not get the outcome they wanted, they will accept the decision if it is seen to be fair. If it was not a fair process, expect to see rearguard actions aimed at undermining the decision.

A fair process involves the relevant parties properly. That does not mean sending out a brief questionnaire and then ignoring the results. As with Martha and the tribal elders, it means taking time to talk it through. Time apparently wasted on making the decision is gained on implementation. As soon as the decision was made for Martha, a group of the locals marched into the bush with her to find a location for her hut and to build it for her.

CHAPTER 22

BEYOND HONESTY AND INTEGRITY

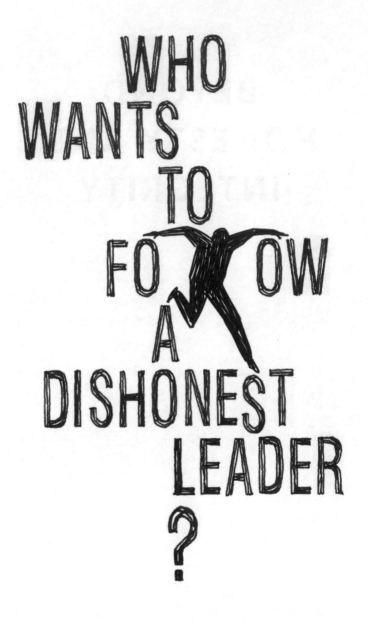

Honesty and integrity are not just important qualities, they are highly divisive. Any leader who was rated low on honesty and integrity was rated low on everything else. Only if they passed the honesty and integrity test did they stand a chance of being rated well on any other factor. At first, this seems obvious: who wants to follow a dishonest leader?

But history is full of leaders who have been scumbags. Dictators, conquerors, megalomaniacs and mass murderers have done more than their fair share of shaping history. For better or worse, people like Stalin, Hitler and Mao shaped the 20th century: only their most fervent apologists would claim that these dictators scored well on honesty and integrity.

So do leaders really need honesty and integrity?

The puzzle was solved in an unlikely place: the plush London offices of an investment bank. The banker was holding forth about the importance of honesty and integrity. When asked if he expected anyone to believe that an investment banker could have honesty and integrity he smiled the way a shark might smile at a seal: he was ready for the kill.

"Honesty and integrity have nothing to do with morality or ethics," he said, gaining credibility immediately. "It is much more important than that. It is about trust. If my team does not trust me, they can walk across the road today. If clients don't trust me, I have no clients. And an investment banker with no team and no clients is no use."

Finally, this makes sense: trust is essential for any leader. Even the most evil of leaders are trusted by their followers: they need loyal henchmen to do their dirty work.

But this raises another problem: how do you build trust?

You need to do three things to build trust.

First, you have to be reliable. Always deliver. Trust is like a vase: once it is broken, it is very hard to put back together again. And weasel words will not help: "I will try . . . do my best, I hope . . ." all give you escape clauses if you don't deliver. Except that what you say and what is heard is different. Your promise to "do your best" will be taken as "I will . . .". So if you want to remain credible, manage expectations well. Under-promise and over-deliver is far better than over-promise and under-deliver. Have a difficult conversation about expectations early rather than make excuses later on.

Second, show you have some common interests, common priorities and common values. In business and in tribes, we prefer to work with people who are like ourselves. This is not good news for diversity. Look at many top companies and they all value the "one firm firm" or "our way". Regardless of ethnicity, faith or sexuality, they want people who think alike and have common values. If you want to build trust, you have to build rapport: build a bridge across to the other person.

Finally, manage risk. You may trust a stranger to give you directions to the next town. You probably would not trust the same person with your life savings. Risk is the soft underbelly of trust. If you want someone to trust you, make it easy for them. Start with little commitments which are easy to give, and build slowly from there.

CHAPTER 23

DEALING WITH CRISES

Great crises produce great leaders, all the way from Moses to Churchill. Crises are the moments of truth which separate out the leaders from the rest. And in any business career, there are always plenty of crises. So do not shy away from crises: they are your chance to shine and to make a difference. And if the crisis is self-inflicted, it is your chance to save yourself. Since we know there will be crises, it pays to know how to deal with them.

Laars Matthis, a Saami reindeer herder, gave a perfect example of how to handle a crisis. We were herding the reindeer on their annual migration, when one of the family fell through the ice. Her outer clothes protected her, but water came over and into her boots. Arctic boots are very good at keeping water out most of the time, but when water gets in, it stays in. And it was cold: our thermometer went down to −20 centigrade. It was a fat use: the temperature never got that high. So even after we pulled her out of the ice, she faced the prospect of wearing a wet boot, which rapidly becomes a block of ice, which leads to loss of the foot. This is not good.

Meanwhile, the migrating reindeer were doing their own thing. They were rapidly scattering over the horizon in search of food. If your entire wealth are your reindeer, this is not good either. So what did Laars Matthis do?

First, there was quite a lot he did not do. He did not panic. He did not get angry. He did not start the blame game or the inquisition into what went wrong and why we were on the wrong bit of ice. He did not try to delegate away the problem to someone else and he certainly did not ignore the problem.

He focused on the most important thing first: the freezing foot. It would take hours to herd the reindeer back, but at least they would not die. As it happens, he had brought with him some dry grass from the summer season: out of this he fashioned a dry inner boot liner which removed the immediate problem. After that, he re-gathered his herd. Crisis over. Experience and preparation count: the more you have seen of crises, the better prepared you become.

Every crisis unfolds in its own messy way. But there are consistent principles in how you can react well or less well, as follows:

Ineffective crisis response	Effective crisis response
Start the blame game	Find a solution
Fight fire with fire: get angry	Be positive and calm

Ineffective crisis response	Effective crisis response
Analyse what went wrong	Move to action
Deny the problem	Recognise the problem early
Panic, give up, be overwhelmed	Focus on one thing at a time. Make it simple
Do it yourself	Get help

The more experience you get of dealing with crises, the better you become at dealing with them. So do not run from crises. Embrace crises and use them as a chance to develop and to stand out from your less courageous peers.

CHAPTER 24

DEALING WITH CONFLICT

Wherever you have humans, you have conflict: competition for food, for money, for women, for land is endemic. Normally the competition is civilised, occasionally it is brutal.

Organisations are set up for conflict.

For speed readers who may have missed the point: organisations are set up for conflict. Organisation theory focuses on how organisations build cooperation. But theory and reality are often strangers in the world of management.

As we have already seen, most organisations consist of competing tribes. Finance, HR, sales, IT, Japan, Europe, the USA, top and middle management will all have their own windows on reality. Each function and geography earnestly believes that their priorities are the most important. Each one will be fighting for a limited pot of organisational budget, management time and promotion opportunities. It is through this messy process of conflict that organisational priorities are often decided. And when things go wrong, it is suddenly open season for conflict between the tribes of the organisation.

So when things get hot, how should you react?

The normal human reaction is to rise or fall to the level of those around you: if they get angry, you get angry. If they start blaming, you start blaming. This does not move things forward. In practice, there are some basic principles to follow:

- Focus on the outcome: do you want to win an argument or win an ally?
- Remain positive: you will be remembered for how you behave
- Listen and empathise: it is very hard for people to remain angry when they are being listened to
- Only deal with the issue when the other side is calm and ready to listen
- Avoid blame

Finally, how do you remain positive when everyone else is being negative and hostile? Remember, the moment you join in the game of making snide remarks, you give the other side the chance to crawl out of the gutter and get on their high horse by highlighting your negative behaviour. You have to wear the mask of leadership and be the role model others want to follow. When the immediate conflict is over, you will be remembered more for how you behaved than for the merits of your argument. No one, least of all your boss, cares for the "I said, he said, but we meant, anyway they didn't . . ." discussion. All your righteous indignation will achieve is to throw more fuel on the fire.

It does not matter what your personal trick is for staying calm, as long as you have one and it works.

CHAPTER 25

FOCUS FOCUS FOCUS

Top leaders are not always nice people. Think of the great dictators of the 20th century, from Stalin to Pol Pot. Besides massive ambition, they all tend to have obsessive focus on what is most important to them.

When Churchill was leading the British war effort, penicillin was in scarce supply. In June 1942, the US had enough stocks to treat 10 patients. As supply began to grow, the question of priorities came up: who do you treat first with this life saver? Who would you prioritise for treatment with the new wonder drug:

(a) soldiers who had received serious wounds in combat, and needed large amounts of penicillin?

(b) soldiers who had caught syphilis on leave, but needed a little penicillin to return to active service?

Churchill was clear: the only thing which counted was winning the war. That meant getting as many soldiers fit for combat as fast as possible. The wounded war heroes on the North African front would have to take their chances, because they could not take the penicillin. The penicillin was used to sort out syphilis and get soldiers back to the front line fast. Cruel but necessary.

Sixty years later, I found myself in the middle of the Libyan sahara. I asked my Tuareg guides to draw a map of their territory. It was a simple map with just three things on it. I asked them about each item:

"What's this?" I asked about an odd looking structure.

"You asked what is important in our territory," replied the Tuareg. "Well, we are in the middle of the Sahara. So water is important, and that is a well."

"And this?" I pointed to some palm trees.

"This is the Sahara. We need water. Palm trees go with an oasis. That is an oasis."

Then I pointed to some bags and asked about them. The Tuareg looked exasperated: "Let me explain. We are in the Sahara. We need water. Those are bags. Water bags. For water."

The Tuareg had 100% focus on what was important to them: water.

In business it is exceptionally hard to maintain focus. The management marathon is one where you have to juggle twenty items at the same time while running faster and faster just to stay still. The noise

of day-to-day crises and deadlines drowns out everything else. But good leaders achieve focus: they
create clarity out of fog. I am yet to hear a top
leader call for less focus.

Here are two questions to help achieve focus:

1. What am I doing that is relevant to bosses at
   least two levels above me?
2. What will I do this year that I will remember in
   ten or twenty years time?

Neither of these questions can be answered by
the number of emails you send, the meetings you
attend or the amount by which your salary increases.
In ten years time, you will remember none of these
things. Of course, you have to deal with the day-
to-day noise of management. But focus on the one
or two things where you can make a difference to
your firm and yourself. Then you are on the path
to leadership.

CHAPTER 26

ALIGN YOUR TRIBE

Some warriors sat down and drew a map of their tribal territory. It was a bloody map. Tribes fighting against each other; walls and barricades being erected to defend territory wherever possible. They showed the map to their tribal chief who was aghast. He saw that the bloodshed did not come from wars with other tribes: it came from warring factions within his own tribe. At that moment, he knew the survival of his tribe was at stake: he had to act fast.

The tribe in question was not a traditional society. It was the Central Bank of a very large country; the warriors were some senior officials and the chief was the Governor of the bank.

In many ways the result was typical of what happens when a firm maps its territory. The divisions become obvious; no one seems to be able to see the outside world of threats and opportunities which exist beyond the tribal boundaries of the firm itself. In contrast, when tribal communities draw maps of their territory, there is complete unity within the tribe and great clarity about the external threats and opportunities they face. Lack of clarity and internal rivalry are luxuries which you cannot afford when you are living on the edge.

Neither a firm nor a tribe which is fighting itself is likely to survive. But within a firm, there will always be rivalry between functional groups, business units, geographies, products and even levels of the organisation. So a large part of the leadership challenge is to create alignment across the firm.

The tribes give some clues to businesses about how you can create alignment:

- Have a very clear and compelling vision: avoiding extinction is both simple and clear. Everyone can align themselves behind that.
- Avoid individual rewards and bonuses: these are a sure fire way to guarantee divisiveness and rivalry.
- Encourage physical proximity: it is hard to fight people you talk to every day.
- Celebrate together. Tribes dance together, eat together and celebrate individual and group rites of passage together.
- Have clear and uniform values which exist in actions and in reality, not as a paper document. The leader should be the standard bearer for the values.
- Ditch the slogans: if you act the right way you do not need the figleaf of motivational posters and messages to cover up for the lack of alignment.

Firms have an advantage over tribes in creating alignment. They can recruit selectively and to type; they can enforce common standards and systems; they can use common methods across the firm. Many of the most successful firms today pride themselves on their internal unity; they will talk explicitly about the "One firm firm" (Mckinsey), "The Toyota Way" or "Blue Box thinking" (American Express).

The adage "united we stand, divided we fall" holds true for all firms. The leader has to make sure all noses are pointing in the same direction.

CHAPTER 27

HOW TO GET UP IN THE MORNING

How do you get up in the morning? Here are three ways:

1. Wake up in the middle of wars, famine, disaster, greedy businessmen, lying politicians and widespread scandal. This is called waking up to the morning news.
2. Wake up and walk three miles through the bush to a muddy creek to collect some water. Collect some brushwood on the way back. Wash and cook with what you have collected. Then start the day's work. That is daily reality for many tribes.
3. Wake up to a miracle: turn on a tap and find cold running water comes out, and you can drink it. Turn on another tap and another miracle: the water is hot without collecting brushwood. Listen to some music, go to work with time to spare.

When you start the day stressed, it is hard to recover. So start the day the way you mean to go on. When you wake up to a couple of miracles each morning, it is more or less impossible to have a bad day. Being positive becomes a state of mind, not a slogan. But it is difficult to recognise just how extraordinary our ordinary has become. It is hard to see what is familiar: we take it for granted.

Good leaders spread hope, not gloom. And you cannot spread hope unless you are positive yourself. We all have our routines: choose the routine which lets you start the day in the right frame of mind.

CHAPTER 28

KEEPING
CONTROL

When leaders talk about control they will often speak at length about core corporate systems such as:

■ Information management and reporting systems
■ Financial and management accounting systems
■ Reward and measurement systems
■ Standardisation of procedures and processes
■ Audit and governance

All of this would be sophisticated nonsense to the ears of tribal people, who simply would not know what any of it meant. And yet it is clear that most of them have very high standards of control: there is not much deviancy within any tribe. So there must be something else which they do to achieve control.

In practice, there are two other sorts of control that leaders can learn from history.

First, tribes achieve high degrees of control through cultural compliance. Cultural norms are rigorously set and enforced. Gruesome initiation rites are a down payment on commitment to the tribal way of doing things. Constant public celebration reinforces the right behaviours. And peer group pressure is a very effective way of avoiding delinquency: no one wants to be the person who let down everyone else.

A strong and cohesive peer group will be largely self managing. The empires of the past depended on cadres of like-minded people going to far-flung places and upholding the standards that had been inculcated into them in their homeland. The public schools of Britain were training grounds for the officials of Empire.

Second, history shows that control through skills and standards can be highly effective. The guild movement throughout the Middle Ages was based on enforcing common standards and common skills. In theory, this was for the public good; in practice, each guild became a closed shop and stifled both competition and innovation. Control through standards and skills still exists in the major professions such as law and medicine, with roughly the same impact as on the medieval guilds.

For leaders, these traditional forms of control provide a welcome alternative to the normal bureaucratic methods of corporate control. Most management control systems enforce compliance and are based on a large degree of mistrust.

Cultural compliance and peer group pressure are more flexible and encourage commitment, not just compliance. From the leader's perspective, this requires showing more trust, reducing the focus on formal control mechanisms and measuring outcomes rather than measuring details of the process.

Some leaders believe you cannot reduce corporate control systems without chaos resulting. Ricardo Semler, who runs the Brazilian company Semco, proves that you can let go and succeed. He allows individual team members to select their managers, set pay rates, set terms and conditions and make all the major decisions. When you have the right culture, corporate controls become an expensive overhead.

All leaders must exercise control, but we have choices about how we exercise that control.

HOW TO LEARN
TO LEAD

Chief John looked like a chief. He wore huge bird of paradise feathers in his head dress, and his body paint was more elaborate than anyone else's. He even had a throne: a rickety old chair which was the only chair in the entire village. The conversation turned to who would succeed him as chief eventually. Chief John thought about it.

"Well," he said, "it will be up to the village to decide. But they will, of course, choose my son. Since he was born he has seen me settle every dispute. He knows all the characters and how to deal with them. He knows every dispute, every agreement, every promise. He is the living record of our society, so of course the village will want him as the chief."

Chief John was training his son to be the next chief, in the best tradition of the hereditary democracy, if such a thing can exist. The training was not about books and courses. No one could even read or write. The training was about carefully nurturing the right knowledge and experience.

In the business world I often ask groups how they learn to lead. I give them a number of possible sources of learning to lead, from which they can pick two. Which of the following six ways of learning to lead have been most important to you?

Books
Courses
Bosses (good or bad lessons)
Peers/colleagues
Role models (inside and outside of work)
Experience

Most people are like Chief John: they rate their own direct experience and the experience of others far above books and courses. This makes sense: experience is more credible and more direct as a way of learning. But it also carries a fatal flaw: it turns your path to leadership into a random walk. Good experiences and bosses accelerate your career, poor experiences become a career dead end.

So how do you turn the random walk of experience into the high road to leadership? A career should be a noun, not a verb: you do not want to career uncertainly through your life. Here are four things you can do:

Make sure you get the right bosses, roles and experience. Do not leave your future to the tender, but random, care of HR. Negotiate your future.

- Keep a notebook. Experience is about copying things which you see being done well, and avoiding mistakes which others make. Use a notebook to record your learning: over the years you will create your own success manual.
- Use books and courses: they will not tell you the answer, but they will help you create some sense out of the nonsense which you encounter in business life.
- Find a coach. Some are good, some are not. Weak coaches answer every question with a question. Good coaches add insight, give support, challenge and accelerate your learning from experience.

LEADING THE ORGANISATION

INTRODUCTION

Leadership is not just about your personal skills and qualities. It is about how you deal with your organisation, whether it is a small departmental team, a global firm or a tribe.

In some areas, it is very obvious that we can learn from the past and learn from tribes. Business leaders often make big talk about "competitive warfare". That simply shows how little they know about real warfare. If you lose a business battle, you might lose money. If you lose a tribal battle, you lose your life. This gives an intensity and focus to tribal competition which ensures that they are very practical.

In other areas, it is less obvious what we can learn from the past. Information systems in the tribal world consist largely of gossip, word of mouth and celebrations. And their technology is either primitive or completely absent. But that is the point. When we see how organisations survive without these luxurious necessities, we see more clearly how we both use and abuse the resources we have.

Finally, there is one surprising message from the tribes, which resonates with anyone struggling with the pace of change. It is a truism that the pace of change is faster than ever. This is one of those eternal truisms, like the past was always better and the youth of today are always dissolute. Like those truisms, it is largely untrue. At first sight, most tribes seem to be preserved in aspic. Nothing could be further from the truth. In reality, they are all changing and changing fast: some because they want to, others because they have to. In many cases, they face a simple choice: change or die. And much of the change can be radical. The way they cope with change illustrates some of the best and worst of how we can manage change today.

CHAPTER 30

THE ART OF UNFAIR COMPETITION

The problem with a fair fight is that you might lose it. History shows that it is not the taking part that counts: it's the winning. History is written by winners, not losers.

The Laikipia have a tradition that each new cohort of young men must prove their worth by killing a lion. This sounds like a true test of courage: taking on a lion in unarmed combat is the sort of fight which the lions enjoyed more than the Christians in ancient Rome. The Laikipia warriors may be brave, but they are not stupid. They kill their lion by approaching it unseen from downwind, and then they shoot it with a poisoned arrow before retreating to the nearest lion-proof tree. After a while, the lion dies from the poison. The warriors cut off its tail and they go back to the village for some nasty initiation rites. They have shown the qualities of the true leader: they are smart, not just brave. The fight is, of course, entirely unfair on the poor lion. And that is the whole point: if you fight, be sure to win.

If you are on the wrong side of unfair competition, disaster strikes. In the highlands of Papua New Guinea we came across a village which had been burned to the ground and the crops destroyed. These are not good memories for a child to grow up with. The village had been attacked by an overwhelming force while the men were away at market. It was a completely one-sided attack.

Every business needs a source of unfair competition. It is only here that the business can earn the "excess profits" that enable it pay for all the failures, long-term investments and setbacks which inevitably befall any firm.

For a business, an "unfair" advantage is one that no competitor can easily copy. Most successful firms have such an advantage. For instance:

- Oil firms: licences to drill in areas of low cost production
- Pharmaceutical companies: patents on medicines
- Utility firms: embedded infrastructure with no natural competition
- Banks: sticky customer base: you are more likely to change your spouse than change the bank in your life
- Retailers: best location on the high street or shopping mall

- Brands: Nike, Louis Vuitton, Coca Cola are never going to be copied
- Software: virtual monopoly on desktop operating systems (Microsoft)

If your firm talks about "points of differentiation" be very worried. Things like packaging, pricing and many product features are very easy to copy.

What is your source of unfair competitive advantage?

CHAPTER 31

COMPETITIVE STRATEGY: ASYMMETRIC WARFARE

We have seen how most tribes and firms do not care for a fair fight. When the Laikipia go cattle raiding, they always pick on a weak village and pick a time when all the men are away. And they attack in force. It is not pretty, but it is effective.

But you cannot always guarantee an unfair advantage. So what do you do when you are faced with a far stronger opponent? This is the challenge every start up faces when taking on entrenched competition and an established market leader.

The obvious thing is that you do not take on your opposition on their terms. You fight on your terms. You learn from how David dealt with Goliath. In a straight fight, the giant Goliath would have crushed young David. So David picked up a sling and felled Goliath with a stone from his sling. That was not the fight that Goliath was expecting. This basic lesson in asymmetric warfare has lasted to this day, in the way that guerrilla forces tackle conventional forces or the Taliban oppose the coalition in Afghanistan.

As in war, so in business: more men, money and technology does not guarantee success. But overcoming a stronger opponent requires some creativity. Here are six classic ways in which you can be creative and find an asymmetric advantage over an incumbent.

- Copy someone else. Ryanair and EasyJet have overtaken established airlines by copying the discount airline model from the USA and South-West airlines. No insight but lots of courage and effort required.
- Exploit a new technology. Kodak dominated photo processing. Kodak Chrome is no longer produced, put out of business by digital photography.
- Build a new economic model. Google ousted Yahoo!, AOL and other early search leaders not by having a better search engine, but by having a better economic model: paid search instead of subscriptions or banner advertising. Obvious, but only with hindsight.
- Occupy new territory. Incumbent telecoms operators were natural monopolies in the days of land lines. Vodafone and others outgrew them without even having to compete, by occupying the new land of mobile telephony.
- Exploit an under-served market segment. This is how Canon, a puny outfit at the time, took on the mighty Xerox. Xerox was addicted to high

end copying. Canon produced small copiers that could be bought, not leased and could sit in each executive's office and bypass the central copying function. Xerox ignored Canon until it was too late.

■ Change the rules of the game. Henry Ford proudly offered the Model T in "any colour, as long as it is black". His idea was to reduce costs, mass produce and make the car available to the masses. It succeeded until Alfred Sloane at GM introduced the idea of "A car for every purse and purpose". Sloane introduced market segmentation: move beyond price and give different types of customer what they want. It nearly killed the monolithic Ford.

In every case, there is a simple message: a good idea beats the dull weight of money every time. Incumbents are risk averse. They stick to their proven success formula and normally react to the new challenge only when it is too late.

How will you slay your Goliath?

CHAPTER 32

WHEN TO FIGHT

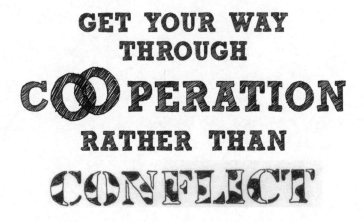

GET YOUR WAY
THROUGH
C**OO**PERATION
RATHER THAN
CONFLICT

Modern corporate life is full of battles. The obvious battles are between firms for sales and market share. The less obvious but more vicious battles are the battles within firms. The battles for promotion, for management time and support, for budget, for the right assignment and the right staff, for avoiding blame and gaining recognition are all familiar to the corporate warrior.

Some of these battles are necessary, some are not. The effective leader knows which battles should be fought and which should not. The Chinese philosopher Sun Tsu, writing over 2500 years ago, gives today's leader a useful guide on which corporate battles to fight. He laid out three rules of warfare in his book *The Art of War*:

■ Only fight when there is a prize worth fighting for
■ Only fight when you know you will win
■ Only fight when there is no other way of achieving your goal

In other words, fighting is pretty much the last thing the corporate warrior should do: it is better to get your way through cooperation than conflict.

All of Sun Tsu's three rules are relevant today:

- Only fight when there is a prize worth fighting for. Some battles are essential for survival and success: getting the right job, promotion, budget and team are must-win battles. Other corporate battles over status, priority and perceptions are little more than the ritual rutting of stags.
- Only fight when you know you will win. Generals reckon that most battles are won and lost before the first shot is fired. The side with the best position and resources is set up to win. So make sure that you have all the key stakeholders supporting your position early. Normally, that stops anyone fighting you, because they know it will be a lost cause.
- Only fight when there is no other way of achieving your goal. Collaboration is better than conflict. Find ways in which you can align your agenda with those of your colleagues; get support from a powerful sponsor such as the CEO; minimise the perceived threat of your idea to other people; work your networks.

Next time you see a corporate battle looming, apply the Sun Tsu test to the problem. You will find that most corporate battles fail one, and sometimes all three, of his tests: they are pointless. And even if you win the battle, you lose an ally. In the course of a long career you do not want to make a habit of acquiring enemies. Leaders need allies, not adversaries.

CHAPTER 33

CHANGE OR DIE

Change is a necessity, not a luxury. All organisations change or die, even traditional societies.

If you travel across the Mongolian steppe you will occasionally spot a nomad's yurt, or domestic tent. They all look the same and they all have a small wooden door which always faces due south. It looks like a scene that has not changed for thousands of years. And then you get closer. Outside one yurt you spot a small generator; outside another, a motorbike and outside a third, a satellite dish.

The signs of change are everywhere. In the arctic you can see a small fence running along the border between northern Finland and Norway. Fences mean change if you are a migrating reindeer: reindeer are good at many things, but they do not quite get property law or international boundaries. Fences mark a shift from a nomadic lifestyle for the reindeers and their owners to a sedentary and farming lifestyle collecting EU subsidies.

In the bush, Shillingi talked about his life. It was a bloodbath all the way through: attacking other tribes, getting attacked by elephants, killing lions and terrorising the wildlife. And now he spends his life looking after the wildlife. Four years of drought had killed most of the wildlife and his tribe faced starvation. So they decided the only way to survive was to move from killing animals to farming tourists: they had to look after the wild animals so tourists could shoot them, with their cameras. As changes in corporate strategy go, that is about as radical as they come.

Most organisations fail because they cannot change fast enough. Only 28 of the original FTSE 100 firms are still in the index after 26 years. Most have been over taken or taken over inside one generation. The larger and more successful a company becomes, the harder it is to change: dinosaurs don't dance. Successful firms become prisoners of their own success: they develop a business model which works, and if they are sensible they keep on refining it and improving it. Incremental change is less risky than radical change, and all the internal reward and recognition systems are geared to this reality. The best predictor of next year's strategy is this year's strategy, plus or minus a bit. So large firms look strong, but their strength is very brittle. They are highly vulnerable to asymmetric competition: people who come in and change the rules of the game.

As with firms, so with leaders. The more successful a leader becomes, the more set in their ways they become. They have decades of experience to show that what they do works, and they do not take kindly to some coach or academic telling them that, although they may be right in practice, they are wrong in theory.

The successful leader succeeds as long as the world does not change too much. If the world changes, they suddenly look very exposed. To survive as a leader you have a choice. You can focus on one way of working, which will typically be based on lessons learned at the start of your career. These leaders are easy to spot: their leadership style has changed as little as their taste in films or music: they will hark back to the good old days. If you go down this route, be sure to find the context that fits your style and hope it will last until you retire.

Alternatively, try to build some hinterland. Gain new experiences both inside and outside work. Challenge yourself to try new things and experiment. You will learn to be versatile: you will be able to adapt to new circumstances as they arise.

The focused leader can go further faster but is also more likely to crash and burn; the versatile leader lasts longer. Your choice.

CHAPTER 34

CONTROL YOUR OWN DESTINY, OR SOMEONE ELSE WILL

The badlands on the border of Northern Territory and Western Australia show what happens when you lose control of your destiny. Uncle Jack is a leader of one of the aboriginal communities in the area. He was dismissive of the aborigines who had drifted to town: "Drink, drugs and dice. Then death. That's their problem," he said.

The journey to drink, drugs and dice was not what the aborigines had planned. After the war, the Australian government decided to help the aborigines by civilising them: that meant taking the children away from their parents and putting them into special schools. Inevitably, there was much good will and much abuse as well. The girls would be put into domestic service and the boys would be set to work on ranches, for no more than board and keep. Eventually, the government realised that such exploitation was unacceptable, so they insisted that the aboriginal labourers were paid a proper wage. So the aborigines all got turfed out of work: the ranchhands were replaced by cars and helicopters and domestic staff were simply unaffordable.

So the aborigines were left without work and without any family to fall back on: they had lost their original parents. So the government stepped in again and put them on the dole, where they had nothing to do but drink, drugs and dice. Good intentions at every stage led to disaster: at no point did the aborigines have any control over their own destiny.

At least in the case of the aborigines the government had benevolent intentions, even if the outcomes were a disaster. In planet business your HR department may be benevolent and efficient, but do not hope to get lucky with their assignment process: hope is not a method and luck is not a strategy.

As a leader you have to control your own destiny. At the minimum that means:

■ Find the right employer and right boss
■ Find the right assignment
■ Manage expectations
■ Make sure you have the right support: team, budget, resources

It is your career: no one else will care about it as much as you do.

CHAPTER 35

LEADING CHANGE

Leaders talk about change, but are not very good at it. The track record of the world's top firms show that most fall by the wayside within one generation: from global domination to oblivion in 25 years. They do not fail because the leaders become dumb. They fail because they are unable to change with a changing world: new technology, new business models, new competitors come in and change the rules of the game. The giants find it hard to abandon the success formula that had served them so well in their growth phase. Their success formula turns to poison: first the formula fails to work and then it kills them.

Leaders have to lead change. The challenge is to know how to set real change up for success. The tribal world has even more compelling reasons to change, but they have to change without the advice of change consultants. So they do the right thing, because their lives depend on it. And they can achieve radical change.

For instance, the villagers had a dream: education, health and water for all. They also had a nightmare: for four years in a row, the rains had failed. All the animals around them were dying and they knew that they would be the next to die. Change was a matter of survival.

Their big idea was that, instead of hunting animals, they would care for them in the hope that the animals would attract tourists. Moving from hunting animals to farming tourists is about as radical as you can get in terms of corporate strategy. So they put together a group of elders to lead the change effort: everyone was consulted and everyone was involved in the change.

The village elders knew nothing about the theory of change, but they had adopted a textbook approach to change. Some change efforts succeed, and some fail. Success and failure can be predicted confidently with a simple tool: the change equation. The change equation says that for change to succeed, you need four things in place:

■ A vision of the benefits change will deliver
■ A need for change
■ The capability to make the change happen
■ Risks which are lower from moving on than standing still

This applies equally in the tribal and business worlds as shown below.

	Shillingi's world	Business world
Vision of change	Education health and water for the village	Better prospects for the business, department and individual: build a clear business case
Need for change	Drought was killing all the animals the village hunted	Make sure you are dealing with the right problem: important and urgent for the business and top management
Capability to change	Whole village involved and consulted	Ensure you have the right team, right budget and right political backing
Risks of changing versus not changing	Change or die	Manage the rational business risks as well as the personal and political risks of change

Risk is often thought of as logical, rational risk. For the firm, the costs and risk of change are fairly easy to identify. You can find plenty of people on your staff who will happily make their career out of developing a risk log and an issue log for you and then meet regularly to monitor the issues and risks and produce mitigating plans. Such work is both harmless and expensive. But the real costs and risks are not corporate: they are personal:

- What will this change mean to me?
- Will I have a new role, new job, new targets?
- Will I survive the reshuffle?
- How much time and effort will this take?
- If this change fails, then do I go down with it?
- Is this a bandwagon to join or a sinking ship to desert?

Change is not just about systems, structures and strategy. Change is about people. The change equation is a simple way of judging whether your change effort is set up for success or failure.

CHAPTER 36

INFORMATION MANAGEMENT: GOSSIP VERSUS COMPUTERS

At first glance traditional societies do not have much to offer in terms of information management. Many of them remain in places where you can still disappear off the known world: you exist beyond the reach of the internet, mobile phones and computers.

Information management in most tribes seems to consist of gossip. Gossip in the market place, gossip while working the fields, gossip while playing games with stones, gossip while walking. It is a 24/7 sort of information system in which everyone knows exactly what everyone is doing and how they are feeling.

Of course, business leaders don't gossip. Do they?

Business leaders have increasingly sophisticated information management systems at their disposal. Real-time reporting on performance, ever more detailed breakdowns of costs, profits and performance by department, business and customer are becoming routine. The business world is hooked on information: the more information there is, the more the addiction is sated and fed at the same time.

And yet when it comes to finding out what is really going on, what do leaders do? They spend a large amount of time walking around and talking to people to find out what is happening: leaders trust what they hear and see more than what they read. They value informal information systems over formal information systems. Just like tribal people, they gossip.

Everyone has learned how to play games with formal information systems. Leaders use information just like lawyers do: to make a point, not to find the truth. Information is always prejudiced. So the search for unbiased and unfiltered information becomes essential to survival. And that means getting out and talking to people. Leaders know that they have to get beyond the information to find the insight: insight may come from looking at a spreadsheet. More often it comes from talking to people.

Leaders learn to put this behaviour to advantage. They do not try to persuade each other with mountains of data. When was the last time you saw Presidents and Prime Ministers sitting down and presenting PowerPoint and Excel spreadsheets to each other? If a leader tried that, they would be laughed into oblivion. Leaders persuade each other by sitting down and talking the issues through face to face, just as they do in the poorest tribal village in the middle of Mali or the C-suite of the largest multinationals. Leaders trust people more than they trust pieces of paper.

So if you are trying to persuade a leader, do not focus on having the most credible presentation. Focus on having a credible conversation that is supported by executives the leader is known to trust.

CHAPTER 37

RESOURCE MANAGEMENT

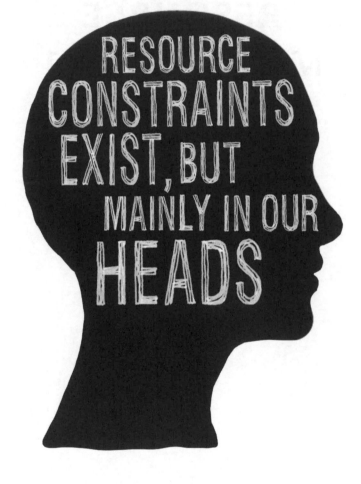

RESOURCE CONSTRAINTS EXIST, BUT MAINLY IN OUR HEADS

What would you do with a scrap of cardboard and some old bottle tops? The kids in the village knew the answer: they made themselves a chequers board. Lack of resources never stopped a successful start up; lack of imagination kills even the greatest firm. Resource constraints exist, but mainly in our heads.

Budget management is one of those basic disciplines all managers learn early in their careers. In larger organisations, the budgets omit the last three zeros: anything less than $1000 or £1000 is simply a rounding error. In the largest organisations, such as government, they omit the last six zeroes. Anything less than a million dollars is a rounding error.

Many tribal families live on less than a thousand dollars a year: they are a rounding error on your firm's HR or IT budget. They learn to make the most of anything and everything. Nothing is left to waste, because they cannot afford waste. Recycling is not a statement of your green credentials: it is a way of life to survive.

In large firms the cost of avoiding waste is often greater than the cost of incurring waste. It costs too much to monitor and minimise the use of paper clips. And some waste is an accepted way of doing business: first class travel and fancy hotels are all part of the deal.

But if you choose to lead outside the comfortable world of the large firm, you quickly discover the merits of tribal frugality. As a start up or a small company you have to make each dollar do the work of two pounds. And there are some surprising discoveries you make:

- It is possible to turn right, not left, when boarding an airplane, without disaster ensuing
- Taxis are not the only form of transport in a city
- You can make your own tea and coffee
- Fresh flowers are not an essential productivity tool
- Cash flow is not an irritating reporting requirement from the Finance Department: it is where you discover if you are going to make payroll at the end of the month
- Creating a brand identity does not require brand consultants, focus groups, a global committee, six months and a million dollars. Give a smart graphic designer a few days and a good brief, and you can get a great result for £1000

It is commonplace for every firm and every leader to say that they are resource constrained. The solution is rarely to throw more resources at the problem. The solution is to go tribal about using resources more creatively and making them stretch much further. You can always do more with less.

CHAPTER 38

INFORMATION TECHNOLOGY AND TRUST

Technology shrinks the world. We know instantly when disaster strikes on the opposite side of the world, and normally have video footage to show it. Within business, video conferencing and email make the most distant suppliers seem like neighbours next door, albeit neighbours with funny work and sleep patterns.

The Roman Empire had fantastic technology: underfloor heating, running water and a functioning road system. Getting a message from one end of the Empire to another would take weeks, even on the best roads. And yet Rome ruled one of the largest empires ever for over 400 years without any of the technology we take for granted.

When Pilate left Rome with the less than attractive brief of running a troublesome backwater called Judea, he was on his own. The good news is that he did not have head office staff calling him every day to explain variations against budget in the salt tax, or demanding an update on the latest aqueduct building programme. And when things went wrong, he had to deal with it himself: he could not call a quick phone conference to get advice on dealing with the latest trouble makers. And if that meant he crucified the wrong person, well . . . whoops. Mistakes might happen, but the Empire kept going.

The Romans governed their Empire successfully because they had something more powerful than communications, technology and sophisticated accounting packages. They had trust. The main players in Empire grew up together and were educated together. They had common values and a common outlook. The same formula has been true of all the old empires, from the Ottomans to the British. They were ruled by a narrow elite which was able to trust each other, even if there were occasional spectacular lapses and misjudgements.

In modern business, technology has become a substitute for trust. The world of hyper-information has become the world of hyper-control. We now know more about each individual and each operation than the greatest dictators, megalomaniacs and control freaks of the past could have dreamed about. And because it is possible to gather more information, we demand more information and we use it. What we gain in terms of control, we lose in terms of individual initiative, trust and accountability. We can no longer do things ourselves: we have to lead by consent and with the support of staff functions, colleagues, suppliers and customers.

But if we want to be good leaders, we cannot lead by analysing spreadsheets, accounts and presentations. We have to lead through other people. A leader without followers does not exist. And no one wants to follow a leader they do not trust. Trust is only built face to face. Success does not come from having the latest smart phone: it comes from building a team that you can trust to perform.

CHAPTER 39

TECHNOLOGY AND PRODUCTIVITY

It is amazing that leaders in the past achieved anything. They had no productivity tools. No internet,
PowerPoint, smart phone at work, or washing
machine, vacuum cleaner or dishwasher at home.
If you find yourself in the highlands of Papua New
Guinea, the nearest market will be a one day walk
away. No roads, no vehicles: you carry your coffee
crop on your back.

And yet some of the greatest leaders are heroes
from the deep past: Julius Caesar, Suleiman the
Magnificent, Genghis Khan. They all achieved
greatness without the help of the latest technology.
So does technology help or hinder a leader?

At first sight, technology helps. We can produce
more work, get more information, travel further
and stay in touch more easily thanks to communi-
cation. But technology has three unintended
consequences:

■ Technology is a distraction, as you find the
   moment you open a laptop in a tribal area.
   The tribe simply comes to a halt so that it can
   admire and play with this new toy. Add a port-
   able printer for photos, and you have a recipe
   for tribal paralysis. Technology can be a attrac-

tive distraction to the real business of work. Personal use of the internet at the office makes the point.

■ Technology does not improve productivity: it raises expectations. Because we can go half way round the world for a one day meeting, we do; because we can produce a 300 page PowerPoint presentation instead of a six page summary, we do; because we can stay in touch 24/7 instead of leaving the office behind us, we do; because we can copy 30 people in on an email instead of sending a note to one person, we do. We not only do these things, we feel we have to. We have not become more productive, we have not become better leaders. We simply do more. But activity is not a substitute for achievement. Leaders focus on what they will achieve, not what they will do.

■ Technology improves communications, not trust. Trust is built face to face, not by email or video conference. Technology helps with transactions: you can share information and issue orders easily. But trust is a low tech/high touch activity which takes time and effort. As we create more virtual and global teams this distinction becomes critical: you cannot manage a virtual team by virtual methods. You still need to build trust and find ways of meeting face to face.

Used well, technology helps leaders. But it can never be a substitute for leadership.

CHAPTER 40

BEYOND RESPECT FOR THE INDIVIDUAL

Respect for the individual is one of the basic values that all firms aspire to today. It is good to respect people regardless of their faith, race, religion, sex or desire to play the accordion. But is it good?

The women of the village were talking beside their mud huts. Somehow the subject of respect for the individual came up. They stopped pounding the millet and turned around in shock. They talked among themselves for a while, trying to understand this new concept. They did not like it at all.

Every traditional society reacts the same way. To them, respect for the individual is a recipe for individualism, politics, strife and selfishness.

And the tribes all believe in something far more important than respect for the individual: respect for the community. The survival of the individual depends on the survival of the tribe, so the community takes precedence over the individual. In affluent countries, the survival of the individual does not depend on the survival of the firm: the firm may go bust but life goes on.

But many of the highest performing organisations command a deep sense of respect from their employees and, more grudgingly, from their competitors and customers as well. In Japan, employees are intensely proud of working for top employers like Sony or Toyota. In the west, the army and many churches have members who are very proud to belong. Even decades after leaving the army or one of these top firms, people still feel a sense of pride in having belonged. So creating a sense of community is important for both survival (for the tribes) and success (for top firms).

Typically, respect for the community is based on four beliefs:

- We are doing something worthwhile: survival for the tribe or fulfilling a mission for other organisations. Give meaning to people for the work they do
- We have high standards – becoming part of our tribe is not easy: try our initiation rites
- We are exclusive – we are not like the other tribes around us
- We have common values and beliefs and we support each other

These beliefs are self-evident if you look at a major church, or the army. But they can also be created within any firm and within any team. As a leader you should be able to make your team realise that they:

- Are doing something worthwhile
- Have high standards
- Are exclusive in that they are unlike other teams and departments
- Have common values and they all support each other

You do not have to attack respect for the individual as a value. That value can remain. You simply offer your team something extra, which is even more compelling: respect for the community.

WHAT'S NEW ABOUT LEADERSHIP

INTRODUCTION

Clearly, the world has changed in the last 200 years since the Enlightenment and the dawn of the Industrial Revolution. Many of the essentials of leadership have survived the massive upheavals since then. But it would be surprising if nothing had changed at all. And leadership has changed.

The changes to leadership are not about the latest breathless theory of leadership to find its way into print. Most such theories last as long as it takes to throw the book in the bin.

Seeing the changes in leadership is not easy. Leadership does not change overnight in response to the latest technology breakthrough in computing. To see what is genuinely new we need to step back and take a longer perspective. Leadership changes like the city: it is hard to see the changes from one day to the next, but over 100 years every city reinvents itself completely. And that is the long perspective we will take to see what is new about modern leadership.

CHAPTER 41

LEADERSHIP IS EARNED, NOT GIVEN

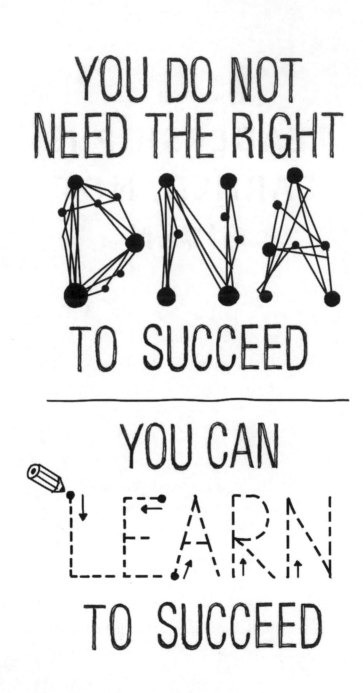

Anyone can lead, if they learn to lead. That is different from the past. Leaders used to be born to lead. If you were the first son of a king, you were likely to land up as king yourself. There was not much by way of a nominations committee when the vacancy finally came up: you grabbed the crown while the corpse was still twitching.

This is good news for leaders. You do not need the right DNA to succeed. You can learn to succeed: there are no magic skills which only a few people possess. Anyone can master the basics of leadership: motivating people, making decisions, crafting a vision, building trust and dealing with crises.

Although leadership is now open to all, the requirements of a leader have changed. The performance bar has risen constantly over time. A simple and revisionist history of leadership will make the point. In terms of a leader's qualifications, this is how the bar has been rising:

- *Medieval world.* Be born into the right family, do not get murdered
- *Industrial revolution.* Be smart. Good IQ counted. Bosses were meant to have the brains and the workers were meant to have the hands. Thinking and doing were separate skills

■ *20th century.* Be good with people (have good EQ, or emotional quotient). Workers got smart and raised their expectations: leaders had to learn to motivate, not simply to command and control

And now the bar has been raised again. Good IQ and EQ are not enough. Leaders make things happen through people and departments they do not control. This requires high political skills: making alliances, building trust, aligning agendas and making the trade-offs that are part of life in flat organisational structures.

Leadership may be earned, not given, but the price is rising all the time.

CHAPTER 42

LEADERSHIP IS ABOUT PERFORMANCE, NOT POSITION

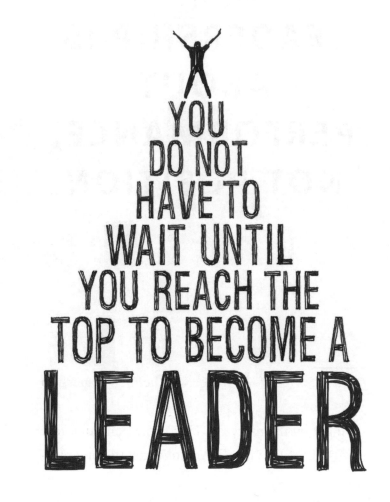

Leadership used to be about the position you held. If you were the king, you were the leader regardless of whether you were good or bad. The only known sanction was murder, but the costs of bungling the murder were painful in the extreme. So most kings kept going unless they were exceptionally evil or incompetent. At every level beneath the king, status determined how much of a leader you were.

This thinking still exists today. People think that if your title says CEO or C- anything else, you must be a leader. This is not true. There are plenty of people with the title of CEO who are not leading: they are simply administering a legacy which was handed down to them.

To understand why this is, we need to know what leadership is. There are thousands of definitions of leadership out there. Perhaps nearest the mark was Henry Kissinger who defined leadership as "the art of taking people where they would not have got by themselves". This is the definition that many CEOs fail: they have not taken the organisation to new places.

The Kissinger definition of leadership also implies that you can be a leader at any level of the organisation. For instance, one of the last people out of the World Trade Centre on 9/11 was William Rodriguez, who had led many people to safety. He passed the Kissinger test of leadership with flying colours. He was one of the building's janitors.

You do not have to wait until you reach the top to become a leader. You cannot afford to wait that long. Anyone can and must lead if they are in charge of a team, department or business unit. An administrator will manage the status quo adequately: a leader will take the team forward, stretch the team to over-perform and do business not as usual.

Only if you learn the habits of leadership early can you hope to lead when you finally reach the C-suite.

CHAPTER 43

LEADERSHIP IS A PROFESSION, NOT A CALLING

Leaders used to lead a community, which might be a kingdom, a tribe or a business in the early days of the Industrial Revolution when owners more or less lived above the shop. This did not always make them good leaders, but it certainly made them committed leaders. Leading was a 24/7 task and they would lead from the front, not from behind a desk in a remote headquarters.

For the most part, leaders could not opt in and out of leading. Leading was not a livelihood, it was their life.

All of this started to change with the Industrial Revolution. Firms became large and complex. The owner could no longer manage the whole firm. In many cases, the owner was no longer a single person. The only way that enough capital could be raised to fund the firm was to seek outside investors. The investors now owned the firm and they needed a hired hand to run the firm for them. Suddenly, leadership had become a profession. Leaders could hop from one firm to another. In the tribal world, tribe hopping is an unimaginable sin: no one can move from one tribe to another. You live and die in the tribe where you were born. That implies a level of commitment which no leader today can give.

Adam Smith noted the effect of this changing contract between the leader and the firm. It is one aspect of the agency problem: the hired agent will never take as much care over a firm as an owner. As Smith wrote: "The directors of such companies, however, being the managers rather of other people's money than their own, it cannot well be expected that they should watch over it with the same anxious vigilance with which the partners in a private copartnery frequently watch over their own."

As Adam Smith noted, professionalising leadership creates a massive conflict of interest. The hired hand will want to maximise his own gains, even at the expense of gains for the firm. In the owner-manager world, there is no such conflict of interest.

This conflict of interest is becoming more apparent with each passing year. Average CEO pay was 50 times average earnings in 1980. Now it is over 500 times average pay. Bank employees continue to receive record bonuses, even though many of their banks would be bankrupt thanks to their efforts, had taxpayers not bailed them out. When shareholders try to regain control over the executive, the media talk with great excitement about a shareholder revolt. How can shareholders revolt when they own the company?

Karl Marx is probably quietly weeping in his Highgate grave. He believed that the workers would rise up and revolt against the exploitation of the owners of capital. Instead, the owners of capital have been reduced to revolting against the workers. The professionalisation of leadership has changed everything.

CHAPTER 44

GLOBALISATION

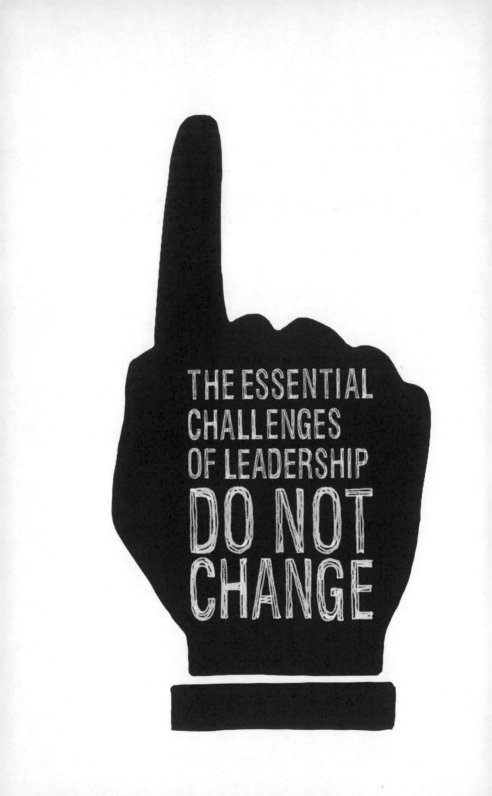

Globalisation does not mean we are all becoming the same. The basic skills of leaders may be universal, but the way you apply them changes around the world. If we want to succeed as global leaders, we have to be able to see the world through the eyes of other people.

For instance, the art of bowing may seem an obscure Japanese custom. Shaking hands is so much simpler in our global world, isn't it? Not necessarily. Try explaining to a Japanese business person the protocol for shaking hands:

- When do you shake hands?
- How do you know when someone is ready to shake?
- How do you show you are ready to shake?
- When do you not shake hands?
- How long and hard do you shake hands and does it depend on who you are shaking hands with?

Suddenly Japanese bowing seems simple: at least there are clear rules about who should bow first, deepest and longest: a quick exchange of meishi (business cards) establishes the pecking order of bowing.

Globalisation brings its particular challenges for leaders. At minimum, it means that leaders earn more air miles and get more tired. Around the world, ways of working change. Pierre-Francois, the Chef du Cabinet in the French government, loved meetings: "They are my chance to sabotage the agendas of other ministries," he declared gleefully. In Japan, decisions are rarely made in meetings: they simply give public confirmation to the consensus reached in private.

Although the etiquette and methods of business vary around the world, the essential challenges of leadership do not change. Followers tend to look for the same five qualities in a leader: having a vision, ability to motivate, decisiveness, being good in a crisis, and honesty and integrity. A leader who can do all of these things well will be appreciated in more or less any part of the world.

Although the substance may remain the same, the style and methods of leadership vary greatly. Even crossing the channel between France and England is to discover very different approaches to leadership. The French take a more autocratic and intellectual approach than the English who tend to be more democratic and practical, to the immense frustration of both sides.

These differences are such that in leadership terms globalisation is a bit of a myth. Most global companies are not truly global in terms of leadership and management. Typically, the top management of most global companies come from the home country of the global firm. Chinese multinationals are run by Chinese; global American firms are run by Americans and global French companies are run by French.

Leadership remains local for the same reason that tribes always recruit their next leader from within the tribe. We may spout adherence to the idea of diversity, but in practice most of us prefer intimacy. We find it easier to work with people we know, who share the same values, same assumptions and same way of working as ourselves. It is an efficient way of working that minimises the chances of misunderstanding. And it makes it easier to gain alignment and agreement across the team.

Firms may be global in terms of reach, but they remain tribal in terms of leadership. If you want to succeed, find the tribe and the context in which you are most likely to succeed.

CHAPTER 45

THE CHALLENGE
OF CONTROL

In the days of kings and queens, taking control was relatively straightforward: once the crown was on your head you were in control. And in absolute monarchies, you had absolute control: the word of the king was law. If you were struggling with control, executing a few aristocrats normally had the desired effect.

When a CEO is crowned, they achieve the semblance but not the reality of control. Large organisations in particular assume a life of their own. The CEO will inherit an agenda which is more or less usable. The CEO also inherits a team which functions after a fashion. The power barons in each division still keep pushing their agendas, and the CEO can survive simply by acting as the referee between all the different factions. Drifting is low risk.

The appearance of control is heightened by technology. All the information that swims across the CEO's desk gives plenty of opportunity for asking questions, offering advice and probing insightfully around variations in budget. The technology can even be used to summon video conferences with under-performing divisions. All of this looks like control and it is control. But it is not leadership.

Let's return to Kissinger's definition of leadership: "the art of taking people where they would not have gone by themselves". This requires a much stronger form of control than simply managing variances and running a tight ship.

To achieve leadership control, leaders need to do two things:

■ Create their own vision
■ Build a team which is willing and able to implement the vision

This is so obvious that it is routinely missed; only six months too late does the new leader discover that they have inherited the wrong vision and the wrong team. By then, it is very hard work to change direction.

Creating a vision is as simple as having a story about the direction in which the firm is going to go. Building the team which is willing and able to deliver is a harder ask.

Building support for the new agenda is a matter of selling and influencing. This will be second nature to anyone who has survived the perils of middle management. And the task is easier than ever because as CEO you hold all the aces: budget control, staffing decisions, pay and bonus, incentive schemes, and the setting of targets and measures. Achieving alignment is essential: without it you are herding cats.

In theory, the management team you inherit should be able to deliver your vision. In practice, new CEOs routinely move their management team around, for the same reason that new kings might indulge in a few executions. The rationale has little to do with improving the overall talent pool. Reorganising is primarily a political act that allows the CEO to exert control over the organisation. Once the power barons realise that the CEO is prepared to move them, they tend to fall into line or they leave the organisation in a huff. Either way, the CEO achieves control.

If you want to lead, do not assume that you are in control because you have an important title. Leading requires taking control actively rather than passively accepting your new role.

CHAPTER 46

LEAD BY CONSENT

The modern corporation is like medieval England. And medieval England was essentially a mafia state. At the top, the don of dons was the all-powerful king. Power flowed personally from the king to the big dons (aristocrats), and knights of the shire whose job was to protect the people; in return they got protection money in the form of tax. And all justice was personal: if you were on the right side of your don, you were looked after. If you fell foul of the don, life would tend to become nasty, short and brutish. It was a method of rule in which consent was passive: as long as the peasants were not revolting, the system ran fairly well. It only got upset when another source of wealth and power emerged: the towns.

As with medieval England, so with the modern corporation. The don of dons is the all-powerful CEO. Like the mafia don, the CEO takes a disproportionate amount of the wealth and rewards. And although there is a formal control system of measures and rewards, in practice control is personal. Anyone who gets on the wrong side of their boss finds that their career becomes nasty, short and brutish. Most bosses tolerate incompetence far longer than they tolerate disloyalty.

Historically, managers have been able to manage with passive consent, just as in medieval England. Command and control was the standard operating procedure: if people did not like it, hard luck.

As with medieval England, the old way of doing things is breaking down as power begins to shift. The power shift is that employees are becoming more and more powerful. They have education, which means that they can do more but also that they expect more. Employees are becoming high maintenance. Critically, employees now have choices about who they work for. The days of the one-factory town are over. If an employer is no good, then a good employee can move with relative ease. And there is a skills deficit: employers are hungry for talent. Even for those with lower skills, there is the safety net of social security. Employers have lost their coercive power. It is no longer possible to lead with passive consent: leaders need the active consent of their followers. Leadership is not just about control: it is about control and commitment.

Firms are struggling with the new world. They still use the military language of command and control, divisions and officers of the company. But as individual leaders we can make our own choice about how we want to lead. We can be old style command and control, which will ensure compliance. Or we can make the effort to build commitment from our followers: show an interest in them, support them, give them meaningful work, help them develop their skills and treat them with respect.

The new way of leadership is harder effort. But it is far more productive than returning to the ways of medieval England.

CHAPTER 47

CHOOSE YOUR TEAM

In the tribal world the leader does not get to choose his (and it is always his) team. The team is the village, which will include the inevitable village idiot. You cannot fire the village idiot: he is part of your team, so make the most of it.

Clearly, as a leader, you have a huge advantage over the tribal leader. You can choose your team. And this is where things go wrong. New leaders typically make two sorts of mistake.

First, they choose the wrong team. As one CEO put it: "I find I hire most people for their technical skills and fire most for their (lack of) people skills." We might add values and political skills to the problem of people skills. This is a classic error. It is easy to hire technical skills, but much harder to select for people skills and values. Because someone with the wrong values and poor people skills is toxic to the team, however good their technical skills may be.

Timpson, who owns a chain of shoe repair shops that bear his name, confronted this problem. He had been hiring cobblers and found that it did not work. They were skilled, but they were often lousy at dealing with customers. So he started hiring explicitly to people skills and values: no technical skills were required at all. He figured that he could train someone in the technical skills of repairing shoes, but he could not train people to be honest, diligent, courteous and kind. The result has been a huge success: Timpson dominates the shoe repair market.

The second mistake leaders make is to drift, to live with the team which they have inherited. Any team changes tend to be enforced, for instance from people retiring or leaving the firm, and replacements are replaced by HR. If you have the B team, you have a recipe for sleepless nights, crises and underperformance. If you insist on building the A team, you will find they make molehills out of mountains before you can start to make a difference.

Pick the team that will help you win.

CHAPTER 48

FIND YOUR CONTEXT

Leaders used to be leaders. If you could lead anything, you could lead everything. Not that there was
much choice: if you were born to be king, you were
born to lead.

Leadership has changed. Leading in one organisation is no guarantee of success in another organisation. If a football manager, conductor and CEO
all swapped roles the results would be entertaining
more than they would be productive. Leadership
has become a much more specialised skill. Leaders
succeed in the context they know: take them out of
context and they struggle. You may as well ask a
cow to play the violin.

And yet the myth of the all-purpose leader sur-
vives. Governments in particular like to hire ex-
CEOs in the hope that some private sector pixie
dust will rub off onto them. It is a forlorn hope.
The track record of CEOs is that very few of them
ever lead a second firm to success. Success is
context-specific.

There are three good reasons why leaders only
succeed in the context most familiar to them:

～ ~ules of the game vary from place to place.
          ıg risk is the lifeblood of an investment
       ᚷer and is kryptonite to a civil servant. Swap

a civil servant and an investment banker round and the results will be ugly.

■ Leaders have to know how to get things done. Inside their normal territory, they know who to call, how the power structures work and they have established a trusted network of colleagues on whom they can rely. Move context and the leader loses that trusted network, has no idea how the power structures work and does not even know who to call to make things happen. The great leader becomes a useless leader very fast.

■ Industry expertise counts: it helps to know the markets, the competition, the technology. In theory, you can read about this in reports. In practice, it takes years to master the reality of the market.

As leaders we have to find the context in which we can succeed.

CHAPTER 49

LEADERSHIP: NO MORE HEROES

History is full of heroes and villains. It makes for a more entertaining read than studying the dry statistics of taxes and trade. The business media are also full of heroes and villains for the same reason: it makes a more entertaining read than dealing with the dull detail of business processes and performance.

But history is changing. We now know that the fate of nations is rarely determined by the brilliance or folly of one or two leaders. For a thousand years, England and France have been rivals. They have produced outstanding people who have been heroes in one country and villains in the other: ask each side what they think of Henry V, Joan of Arc, Nelson and Napoleon. And at the end of the thousand years of heroism and folly the two nations are at almost identical stages of economic and social development. The fate of nations depends on much more than a few great leaders.

In the same way, the fate of firms depends on much more than the conduct of one leader. Firms find it hard to escape the momentum of their existing position and market: market leaders tend to stay in front and firms find it hard to grow in declining markets.

Hamlet said: "There's a divinity that shapes our ends, rough hew them how we may." The fate of most firms is divined by their circumstances; leaders are simply rough hewing that inevitable fate.

Today, business is so complicated that even the most heroic leader cannot do it all alone. Leadership is now a team sport. The lone hero is a myth that is past its sell-by date. Good leaders depend on building a great team around them: business is so complicated that no one can do it all themselves.

The end of the hero leader is good news. Most of us were not born to be heroes. And we do not need to be heroes to be leaders. If we learn our trade, get the right experiences, build our skills and gather the right team, then we can become effective leaders.

Today, we can all aspire to lead. Our destiny is in our hands.

CHAPTER 50

THE LEADERSHIP
JOURNEY

How would you get by without televisions, washing machines, microwaves, cars, internet, computers, mobile phones and all the other modern luxuries we now regard as basic necessities?

People have survived thousands of years without these creature comforts. Bizarrely, they have been happy as well. To find out how this could be I went to Outer Mongolia, which is a vast and empty steppe.

There I met Choimaa, the elderly matriarch of a nomadic family, in her yurt. A yurt is a domestic tent which the nomads can pack up in a day, move and erect again on the same day. It has everything they need, from toothbrushes to horse tackle. And each yurt is laid out in exactly the same way, with the same sparse possessions arranged in the same order around the yurt.

At the end of our long interview I asked her if there was anything she wanted, anything I could do for her. She looked at me in total disbelief.

"Why should I want anything?" she asked. "I have everything I need. I have my friends, I have my family and I have my health."

It is easy to worry about whether we have the latest mobile phone, the coolest car or the best house. Status anxiety puts us into a state of anxiety.

When we get the latest upgrade, we find a colleague who has leapfrogged us and we are back to square one: it is a race we can never win.

It is easy to lose sight of what we are trying to achieve on our leadership journeys. Each of our journeys will be unique, and none of us can tell what the future will be. But whatever your journey is, enjoy it.